THE POWER OF DIVERSITY

MANAGING INCLUSION FOR GLOBAL SUSTAINABILITY

First published in 2023
as part of the Diversity in Organizations, Communities & Nations Book Imprint
doi: 10.18848/978-1-957792-62-0/CGP (Full Book)

Common Ground Research Networks
60 Hazelwood Drive
Champaign, IL 61820 USA
Ph: +1-217-328-0405

Library of Congress Cataloging-in-Publication Data

Names: Casanova, Myrtha B., author. | Barguñó, Javier, author.
Title: The Power of Diversity: Managing Inclusion for Global
    Sustainability / by Myrtha Casanova and Javier Barguñó.
Other titles: El poder de la diferencia. English
Description: Champaign, IL: Common Ground Research Networks, [2023] |
    Includes bibliographical references. | Summary: "Diversity is the nature
    of humanity because the profiles of men and women have highly diverse
    features. The same applies to the structure, behavior and results of the
    groups they form, or the institutions they create and the governance
    tools they use. This evidence has become an axiom of everything that
    concerns humanity. Globalization has brought people and all their
    differences together to act in a unique, dynamically diverse space in
    constant transformation In the nineties, scientists such as Offerman and
    Gowing (IPD, 1996) researched the impact of diversity in the corporate
    communities. The findings again confirmed that global megadiversity,
    when managed, fosters innovation and therefore makes unprecedented
    contribution to the creation of the mechanisms that are driving humanity
    to the highest levels of accelerated development. Diversity and
    inclusion management must be a compulsory course in all education
    systems so that men and women in their professional life leverage this
    core competence"-- Provided by publisher.
Identifiers: LCCN 2023024190 (print) | LCCN 2023024191 (ebook) | ISBN
    9781957792606 (hardback) | ISBN 9781957792613 (paperback) | ISBN
    9781957792620 (pdf)
Subjects: LCSH: Multiculturalism. | Cultural pluralism. |
    Globalization--Social aspects.
Classification: LCC HM1271 .C36713 2023 (print) | LCC HM1271 (ebook) |
    DDC 320.56/1--dc23/eng/20230720
LC record available at https://lccn.loc.gov/2023024190
LC ebook record available at https://lccn.loc.gov/2023024191

THE POWER OF DIVERSITY

MANAGING INCLUSION FOR GLOBAL SUSTAINABILITY

MYRTHA CASANOVA AND JAVIER BARGUÑÓ

COMMON GROUND

To all organizations, institutions, and readers that promote diversity inclusion as an imperative to develop sustainable socio, economic, and political environments in these vulnerable and changing scenarios.

TABLE OF CONTENTS

GRATITUDE

This compendium is the result of thirty years of research, sharing, and working together under the initiative of The European Institute for Managing Diversity (EIMD) A project inspired by John Naisbitt, creator of Megatrends, and Jim Garrison, founder of the World State Forum and the Gorbachev Foundation and presently President of the Ubiquity University. The true authors of this book are Gonzalo Sanchez Gardey, PhD and former Vice-Dean of the University of Cadiz: Margareta Eklund, Secretary General of Working Life Delegations and the EU Social Found Council since 1999 is also Founder of the EU Diversity Charter of Sweden and responsible of the EU regional programs in the Baltic and Balcan countries Jude Smith Rachel, co-Founder of Abundant Sun UK and USA, leader in transformational behavior assessment, and Oscar Palomino, president of Innova-Humana and presently of the European Institute for Managing Diversity. EIMD holds a core commitment to research and modeling strategies to implement diversity and inclusion policies at national, regional, and organizational levels. We fully share that vision and mission to promote diversity inclusion to generate innovations that guarantee sustainable development of any type of organization today and towards the future is highly vulnerable, unpredictable and changing global scenarios.

FOREWORD

New Delhi, 2007, elections to the presidency of the World Engineering Organization. When an assembly of more than 600 delegates, engineers from all specialties, representatives of the professional engineering associations from Africa, America, Asia, Europe, the Commonwealth, and the Arab countries, elected me as president, I became fully aware of the meaning of "diversity." I fully embraced the assertion of, "The power of difference."

I was aware of the need to learn to manage the concerns, talents, feelings, cultures, etc. extremely different between each of the delegates if I wanted to carry out the objectives of my program as the president, after having won with a tight margin.

Myrtha Casanova came immediately to my mind. In 1991, I met the author of the book that today I have the honor to preface. Then, a professor at the (IESE) Business School of the University of Navarra where we had both completed the Senior Business Management Program (PADE) spoke to me about her as a European reference in terms of diversity. I remember asking him: "And what does diversity really means when managing companies and institutions? Is it a barrier or does it add value? What are we talking about when we refer to diversity and its power to move the world?"

As telecommunications engineer, a student of the effect of information technologies on vital and organizational changes, I had followed the publications of research on this topic that began in the second half of the 1980s and crystallized in the early nineties. They overwhelmed me. I began to be aware of the true power of difference; of the abundance of literature on one hand and the lack of practical cases on the other, in order to comply with the multiple dimensions of diversity.

"Myrtha Casanova," the professor told me, "will give you the answers. She will guide you, and will give you light. Talk with her. Debate with her. Myrtha accumulates a very unique practical knowledge due to her ample experience."

He was right. Today, all that practical knowledge, dear reader, is summed up in the book that you have in your hands.

Diversity, Myrtha reminds us, "is the very nature of humanity," and "its management is a critical factor for progress, a resource that must be a fundamental part of a strategy focused on creating inclusive development that fosters social and economic benefits".

The power of difference introduces a kind of difference that extends to biology, sexuality, linguistics, religion, manufacturing models, customers, suppliers, financial sources, technologies used, the capacities of each person in the planet…and it is in this difference where lies the potential for progress. Potentiality magnified by globalization and made possible by the maturity of the technologies of our times.

We all depend on each other. Each form of life depends on other forms of life to advance and only from a knowledge of the value of that diversity and the ability to integrate different visions can a solution be found to the three, four, great questions that humanity faces today.

Let us not forget that, thanks to information technologies, we are all aware of the destiny of everyone.

The power of difference. How can we measure the difference? What is the cost of not managing it and allowing the growth of conflicts? What is the cost of non-inclusion? How are reference companies managing this diversity? Myrtha Casanova analyzes it and responds in her book.

The Power of Difference is, I would say, a treatise, a textbook, academic, perhaps somewhat "tedious" because of the thoroughness with which it explains the evolution of the concept and the analysis of the different dimensions that make up difference. Myrtha duels in all of them, but do not be afraid, dear reader, because each chapter can be read independently. You can stop reading and resume it with equal interest, because it is also a practical manual, full of specific cases with which the author contrasts her reflections.

Myrtha recalls that, even when talking about the science of diversity, there is still no consensus in the academic or scientific community on the procedures, methodologies, metrics for its assessment, or on the correlations between forms of management and their results. So, when the author of this book founded the European Institute for Diversity Management, authoritative voices from around the world praised the initiative.

It covers a notable absence, especially in Europe, which should no longer be delayed. In addition to the major issues, it faced—sustainable development, demographic gaps, unbalanced presence of women in certain economic activities, and the urgent transformation facilitated by digital technologies—she added the urgency to analyze the more effective way to manage diversities, turning difference into a positive factor; to leverage innovation and inclusive progress.

That was the reason for the creation of the institute and the writing of the book, The Power of Difference, which projects her know-how and is a compendium of her personal commitment. Even though in some aspects you may disagree with the author, it is exciting to delve into her reading. The background it brings will guide the reader and respond to concerns about how to act in a subject that, although it is eternal for humanity, today is a consubstantial part of our existence. I encourage you to read it. You will not be disappointed.

Maria Jesus Prieto-Laffargue

Telecommunications Engineer (UPM)
Doctor honoris causa (UPLL)

President of the Spanish Institute of Engineering (2000-2004)
Academic of the Panamerican Academy of Engineering.

CHAPTER 1

The History of Diversity: Source of Conflicts and Innovation

The past has not been either better or worse…It simply has been different. "Better," for people who are resistant to change; a home for life, a job for life, a hobby for life. While "worse," for those who thrive in change; the speed of emerging technologies, virtual communication and its multiple applications, cars that fly, drones that can go beyond human abilities, that deliver in rural areas, or nanotechnology designed for distance surgical interventions, space explorations… Past times must have been a bother for those who love change, who are not afraid of innovation and, in general, hate routine. This is the profile of twenty-first century citizen and beyond. Diversity is the very nature of humanity and, therefore, it is the nature of the global and local scenarios, whether those of the past, the present, or the future. What changes is the dimensions of the diversity in each era.

It is easy to perform in scenarios when their structures are well known; when the causes and consequences of events are clearly understood. The difficulty lies in identifying the causes and then forecasting the effects of the contextual behavior of events. Darwin, with his theory of social evolution, opened the way and invited the scientific world in 1850 to start research on intercultural behaviors. Scientists like Abernathy and Utterback, identified diversity as the critical factor that would single out the twenty-first century.

It was in the eighties that the US corporate community embraced diversity as a key project with the objective of improving the performance of human resources in organizations, a resource that was not yielding the positive results that other resources such as technology and financial management had contributed to the business world. The Conference Board immediately came up with an answer to this growing unrest of the business world and organized a panel to research the impact of diversity in companies.

The Conference Board is a non-profit organization founded in 1916 which currently has over 1,200 public and private corporations as members and is present in sixty countries worldwide. It studies, analyzes, and proposes solutions to optimize the resources that optimize the management and results of business organizations. These three unquestioned key resources which are constantly monitored by the Conference Board are: technology, finances, and people. During the twentieth century, the American corporate world made gigantic strides in the development and use of new technologies, which resulted in extraordinary development leaps in all areas of corporate management. In the same way, new financial management mechanism made a key contribution to US corporate leadership in national and international arenas.

It was an imperative to analyze why human resource management was not contributing as effectively as technology and financial resources had done to corporate results. Traditional human resources corporate policy was based on segmenting people by their differences (with respect to the "norm" of the company) and then designing "positive actions" to neutralize specific problems of those groups of "different people" that created costly conflicts in the organization.

However, this policy did not give the expected results to improve corporate productivity. On the contrary, it rather created increasing conflict. The rest of the staff wondered why they could not enjoy programs equally adapted to their needs. The fact is that the workforce of any company is already diverse in itself because people are different by nature. Decision makers had to take a step forward and learn that segmenting the workforce fostered inefficiency and conflicts; while inclusion of all employees, regardless of their diverse profiles, is the key to generating innovation, and therefore corporate development in present and future scenarios. A constant structure that contributes to the efficiency of the entire process of the organization and therefore is key to its sustainable presence in environment in uncertain constant transformation.

With this objective as a goal, The Conference Board created a panel in which the Fortune 500 companies participated, as well as relevant personalities from the scientific, economic, and academic communities of the country. This rich continuous dialogue went on for a decade; sharing ideas and experiences, testing all kinds of programs and reporting results; building inclusive groups with the objective of stimulating creativity and innovation throughout the organization. The transformation took place, and management shifted from segmenting by differences to understanding that all persons are diverse in one way or another, and that the strategy was to recognizing and respect individual differences in order to manage and promote the inclusion of all members of the workforce. Diversity and inclusion, (D&I) as a corporate policy was born. The companies that participated in the panel began to appoint senior executives who would lead a team responsible for identifying, managing, and promoting diversity in the company. In the corporate organizational chart, this person responded and continues to report directly to the CEO or senior responsible of the organization, generally the position of vice president, because diversity management is not a policy that concerns a specific area or activity of the company. It deals with the transformational behavior of all members of the organization towards acceptance, respect, and inclusion of the differences of others. The objective is to guarantee corporate sustainable development of the organization as a whole in the present scenarios and towards the future.

The scientific community paved the way when in the 1950s and 1960s, it identified "diversity" as the differential factor that would identify the twenty-first century. The academic world was compelled to generate knowledge about this hitherto unknown factor, defining it as an essential element for the management of organizations of all kinds in the new evolving environments. Not only was knowledge developed, but models were also created that would serve as a guide for the leaders of the organizations to establish this policy at corporate level. Diversity and inclusion policy and strategy is based on the transformation of the relational (interpersonal) behavior of all the members of the organization to create an inclusive entity. That is, an organization made up of people of all kinds of profiles who, with their different contributions, experiences and mental schemes, create an innovation and dynamic oriented structure capable of advancing towards the sustainability of the company in turbulent and changing scenarios. The modeling of strategies for the inclusion of diversity became a priority topic of research, design and piloting in the advanced academic world.

The first global study on academic practices in the field of diversity as a corporate strategy was carried out in 2003 at the University of Cádiz under the scientific direction of Gonzalo Sánchez Gardey PhD. Its objective was to identify the universities that were promoting research related to the impact of diversity in production processes, as well as academic projects that were part of the academic curriculum to prepare future leaders for effective business management. At the time, only three percent of the academic world had some type of activity related to diversity at that time.

As the academic curriculum until then did not included diversity as a management subject and the faculty was not prepared to research in order to develop knowledge on the subject, students did not learn diversity inclusion as a basic discipline. Therefore, students joining the work market did not practice D&I in their organizational performance when joining private and public companies.

The European Union Commission is profoundly interested in leveraging the existing diversity in the European space. A clear objective is for Europe to be a major creator of innovation as a desired result of bringing together the very diverse cultures that make up the Union. Directorate General V of Labor and Social Affairs, established the 2000 Directive that regulates the inclusion of diversity as a social, labor, and legal policy in the European Union. The 2000 Directive clearly states that residents in the European Union space have the right to equal opportunity in the access to work life, promotion as well as personal and professional balance, regardless their diverse profiles of gender, ethnicity, age, disability, language, believe, education, and culture in general, besides professional abilities and competence. In 2011, diversity issues passed on to Directorate General of Justice and discriminating in the European Union became penalized by law, Directive which had to be established locally by each member state.

In 2007 and 2008, the European Institute for Diversity Management, together with the European Academy of Business Society (EABIS), EIM Business & Policy Research, the organization for SME research, and Focus Group (UK), carried out a major project across the European Union for DGV. The objective was to analyze the awareness and implementation of diversity management policies by the different agents in the European Union. The results were very alarming. Sixty-three percent of the European corporate world had implemented some action related to the inclusion of diversity and anti-discrimination, although only 0.3% did it as a corporate policy. Small and medium-sized companies in the EU only had a five percent awareness of the importance of the difference in profiles of its people. This is very alarming finding when ninety-two percent of companies in the European Union are SMEs, and which are the once that generate ninety-nine percent of jobs.

As far as innovation is concerned, the result was extremely significant. Eighty percent of the companies surveyed admitted that their creative and innovative capacity was the result of their diverse work teams. Another of the results of the project, "Continuing the Diversity Journey," was the launching of the Diversity Charter: A letter that independent organizations in each country undertake to promote diversity inclusion policies in local companies and towards external agents. The undeniable objective of the Commission is to capitalize the existing military diversity that singularizes Europe as a critical factor to have a prominent role in innovation and sustainability in the global socio-economy.

On the other hand, 9.7% of the academic group reported to include diversity as part of its intelligence research as well as academic activities for students on diversity as a subject. An encouraging increase compared to three percent which was the finding of the research carried out by the Cadiz University in 2003.

The logo of the European Union—a blue rectangle with twelve stars; has a time connotation: the clock that sets "the time" for the Union. It also has a flag with the same logo, a hymn, "Hymn of Joy" by Beethoven, and a slogan: "United in diversity," which was the result of a competition called by the Commission to universities throughout Europe for young students to propose the phrase with which they would like to define what the European Union means. "United in diversity" was the winning phrase, very appropriate for the objectives of the space of peace, dialogue, innovation, and inclusion which is the European Union.

The Diversity in Organizations, Communities & Nations Research Network was founded in 2000 with the vision of bringing together those with shared interests in human differences and diversity, and their varied manifestations in organizations, communities, and nations.

Phillip Kalantzis-Cope, PhD, Chief Social Scientist of Common Ground Research Networks which is the secretariat for the Network, states that the Vision of the Network is to constantly explore the forms and future of human differences and diversities. He points out that "scholarship can be a powerful agent for critical engagement and productive democratic discourse. At a time of considerable change in scholarly communication and publishing, the Diversity in Organizations, Communities & Nations Research Network seeks to challenge the status quo and influence public life. "We are committed to producing and disseminating interdisciplinary inquiry that seeks to educate within and beyond the classroom."

The Network works in partnership with institutions such as the Australian Multicultural Foundation, Deakin University, Charles Darwin University, RMIT University, and the Victorian Multicultural Commission of Australia, the City Council of Amsterdam of Netherlands, the City Council of Montreal, the Ministère de immigration et des communautés culturelles du Québec, and the Québec Immigration, Diversities et Inclusion Department in Canada, the Louisiana State University in New Orleans, the University of the Western Cape, Cape Town, South Africa, the University of Hong Kong, Hong Kong and the University of Ulster, Belfast, UK.

Eugenia Arvanitis (Ph.D.) Associate Professor and Editor, Diversity in Organizations, Communities & Nations Research Network and Director of the Department of Educational Sciences &Early Childhood Education of the University of Patras reports that the main areas of research, exchange, and dissemination of results to organizations, institutions and government at global level which contribute to social and economic sustainability and quality of life and work are the following:

- Dimensions of Individual Differences – Ethnicity, Gender, Race, Socio-Economic, Indigenous, Religion, Sexual Orientation, Disability.
- Dynamics of Diversity – Inclusion, Exclusion, Assimilation, Integration, Pluralism.
- Exclusionary 'isms'– Racism, Sexism, Heterosexism, Ageism, Ableism, Nationalism, Capitalism, Feminism, Anti-Racism, Multiculturalism.
- Inclusive Education – Dimensions of Individual Differences in Learning.
- Educational Policies and Practices – Curricular and Instructional Frameworks for Diversity.
- Ethics in Education – Participation, Inclusion, and Difference.
- Educating Teachers – The Role of Institutions, Administrators, and Community Members.
- Global Frames – Multicultural, cross-cultural, international and global education.
- Planning for Diversity – Inclusive Employment Policies and Practices. Beyond Legislative and Regulatory Compliance – Disabilities, Workplace Harassment, Discrimination.
- Cultural Mediation – Negotiating Assumptions and Practical Outcomes.
- Markets and Diversity – Niche markets, Customization and Service Values.
- Leveling the Playing Field – Global Economics, Fair Trade, Outsourcing, and Equal Opportunity.
- Democracy and Diversity – Questions of Representation and Voice.
- Considering Fames of Justice – Human Rights, Civil Rights, and the Law.
- Capacity Development – Self, Governance and Local Sovereignty.
- Intercultural Relations – Tourism, Travel, Exchanges, Missions.

The Network members organize a worldwide conference each year sponsored by different institutions which represent a broad range of disciplines and perspectives. The Network also supports a book imprint and a collection of journals as well as a constant activity of sharing knowledge, research results, and materials.

Ryerson University's history is rooted in innovative, career-driven education with the goal of addressing contemporary societal needs.

The University of Curaçao is proud of its multicultural character and diverse academic program, that builds local strength for a global future.

The University of Milan Department of Social and Political Sciences 2020 believes that the social sciences in their plurality are pivotal to understanding contemporary political and social systems and processes of change. For this purpose, it promotes multidisciplinary research and innovative and integrated tertiary educational programs.

The University of Granada, founded in 1531, now has over 60.000 undergraduates. With its commitment to high-quality research, the university supports 165 research projects, and the Ministry of Innovation, Science and Business has provided financial support to seventy-eight Projects of Excellence.

The University of Patras was founded in the city of Patras in 1964 and has acquired international prominence for pioneering wide ranging research in areas such as Environment, Health, Biotechnology, Mechanics, Electronics, Informatics, and Basic Science.

The International Institute for the Inclusive Museum is a not-for-profit that subsumes the Pacific Asia Observatory for Cultural Diversity in Human Development established in 2004 as part of the Action Plan of the UNESCO Universal Declaration on Cultural Diversity (2001). It brings together clusters of research and capacity building institutions along with arts, museums, heritage, and environmental agencies across the world. Networking all over the world and with active engagement through social media, the iiiM platform enhances constructive exchanges across research networks and promotes state of the art online research, learning, and teaching systems. A strategic partner with the prestigious Common Ground Publishing, International, Impartial and Independent Mechanism (iiiM) is driven by UN Sustainable Development Goals as defined in Transforming Our World - the 2030 Agenda for Sustainable Development.

Universidad Complutense de Madrid, in 2021 was the Congress organizer. Representatives of universities and institutions from around the world attended the event. Participants debated and exchanged best practices in the creation of research projects that served as a base for the development of intelligence applied to diversity education. The scientific committee in Spain is chaired by Dr. Carmen Miguel Vicente and Dr. Mª Ángeles Medina Sánchez, from the Complutense University of Madrid. Other universities attending the Congress were: the Universities of Jaén, Castilla la Mancha, Salamanca, Murcia, Zaragoza, Chile, Mexico, Italy, Portugal, Italy, United States, India, China, Canada, Australia and Austria, among others.

CHAPTER 2

Nature of Humanity:
Changing Roles of Men and Women

Diversity is the nature of humanity because the profiles of men and women that make up humanity have highly diverse features.

The same applies to the structure, behavior, and results of the groups they form, or the institutions they generate and the tools they create. This evidence has become an axiom of everything that concerns humanity. Globalization has brought people and all their differences together to act in a unique, dynamically diverse space in constant transformation.

In the fifties and sixties, the scientific community established that diversity would be the distinguishing factor of the twenty-first century, with Albermathy and Utterback in the front line, among other researchers. A science of Diversity emerged; the development of intelligence that would be critical to understand and manage as men and women moved forward in search of a sustainable future. In the eighties, the scientific community; Johnston and Packer (1987), among others; not only further researched the concept of diversity, but also established that it would be responsible for the generation of conflicts at global, local, and group levels in the twenty-first century. Later, in the nineties, further analyzing the consequences, researchers such as Cox and Blake identified diversity as the generator of innovation and, therefore, the key factor for organizations to develop inclusive policies that would enhance the value of difference with the aim of turning it into an advantage and not a menace to people and the institutions they create.

On May 20th 2003, Professor Di Stefano from the University of Lausanne and his team presented the results of their research project that fully confirmed the theories published by then. It was definitely established that when people act in random groups, conflicts emerge. Yet when the teams of diverse persons operate with inclusive behavior, innovation and development is the result. This finding became the key for organizations to embrace diversity inclusion policies as core corporate policy, with the clear objective being that of leveraging creativity and innovation to contribute to corporate efficiency and results. Diversity inclusion, creativity, and innovation are therefore the key to corporate sustainability in future highly uncertain scenarios.

The Di Stefano research team based the project in monitoring seventy-two groups of executives operating in complex international environments and selected five countries for the sample: the United States, Mexico, Japan, Germany, and Canada; countries with well identified cultural diversities that have a relevant weight and influence in global environments. Their work went beyond research and developed a training tool they called Cultural Mapping. It is a three-layer program. It starts with extensive interaction between all team members to first explain, then to later accept and leverage their personal cultural experiences and background. The objective is for all the group members to understand the diverse profiles of each of the other team members. The key is to abolish the mind-set which conditions an instinctual reaction to other person's differences. That is, to abolish, if possible, personal attitudes that respond to stereotypes. This makes it easy for them to establish bridges as second step to allow them to share the group intercultural space. In turn, this takes them to the third step, when the group generates very creative thinking and innovative projects, a methodology they name Mapping/ Parenting/ Inclusion.

The stereotypes that determine the attitude of inclusion or exclusion of adults are acquired in childhood. They are not learned, but are integrated and assumed, because children tend to repeat and imitate the behavior of those around them: family, schools, and immediate external environment. Children assimilate and assume what is good and evil, what is beautiful and what is ugly, what is done and what is not done, who the family accepts and who it discriminates against. Without knowing why, they assume and project this behavior towards others; a behavior that then accompanies them throughout their lives. As adults, it is difficult to change these stereotypes. If in childhood, the family rejected or avoided the presence of people of another ethnic group, the adult person will have a first reaction to reject a coworker of another ethnic group, without even giving the opportunity to get to know the person better and to judge his or her qualities. This behavior is extremely serious and continually puts at risk the effectiveness of interpersonal communications, which are essential for the development of the internal process in any type of company, institution, or group of people.

Imagine a child born in China adopted by a German family and lives in Germany since he is two months old. At three years of age, he will speak German.

He has not actively learned it, nor studied it, but has absorbed it and it will be part of its intelligence for the rest of the life. The person unconsciously takes sides, based on the knowledge and behavior imprinted during its childhood. In addition, this unconscious bias attitude towards others has major consequences that condition the social and professional life of persons in their adult lives. Researchers like Dr. Jennifer Eberhardt, or diversity experts like Howard Ross as well as Pamela Fuller, Mark Murphy, and Anne Chow clearly explain this behavior in their books.

Therefore, in order to modify the acquired stereotypes of the persons that work in the organization, companies should organize awareness seminars and awareness programs open to the entire workforce. According to the research of Professor Di Stefano, most of the teams that operate in companies are homogeneous teams whose components share very similar profiles. These groups take the organization to obsolescence, since they tend to repeat past experiences that in new and changing environments are not effective. Employees with different or diverse profiles, groups that cause a great degree of conflict, form the second most numerous groups.

Employees with very diverse profiles make up the third set of groups intentionally. These teams are trained to value the differences of all their members and are responsible for innovation generated in the company.

In the eighties, there were already five diversity councils in the United States and one in Canada under the coordination of The Conference Board, made up of companies from all sectors that had already established their corporate policy to manage the inclusion of diversity. These new policies contributed very effectively to the bottom line. This explains why the United States has been and continues to be the pioneer in innovation in all different sectors. The demographic nature of the country´s population is highly diverse, which facilitates the creation of highly diverse project teams in any company. Companies like Apple, Microsoft, and Google, for example, refer proudly to the diversity of their groups of employees who are responsible for the extraordinary capacity of innovation of the organization.

The United States is a country of immigrants. The first British settlement was established in Jamestown in 1607 and with the arrival of the Mayflower on November 21, 1620 at Cap Code (now Massachusetts), rebelling against the religious discrimination of the King Jacob from England. Immigration has not stopped people from all over the world. The founders knew how to create a land of opportunity, freedom, and hope in which the dreams of entrepreneurs could come true. It is the only country in the world where a black man, born in Hawaii, educated in Indonesia, with an African Muslim father and an American white mother, has been elected president of the nation. Barack Obama, an extremely competent young man, was re-elected for two terms as president of the United States, the most powerful country. A country whose very diverse peoples have contributed to the country´s leadership position in the global technology and socio-economy scenario for the past 200 years.

However, the history of the peoples of Europe has been one of conflicts and wars, until 1957 when five countries signed the Treaty of Rome, which has evolved to what today is the European Union, made up by twenty-seven member states. For the first time in millions of years of history, European peoples are not only not at war, but, on the contrary, for the first time they are building a common space sharing resources, creating wealth and development; thus, occupying a power position in the global scenario. A space that respects the diversity of its peoples: when the four major languages, 200 minority languages are spoken. Although Christianity is the major belief system shared by the EU citizens, many other religions are practiced and respected in Europe, as more and more immigrants from countries from the southern hemisphere immigrate in search of work opportunities and quality of life.

The Commission of the European Union has the clear objective of promoting the diversity of its peoples to turn this resource into a factor of creativity and innovation to compete in technology and innovation in the global scenarios. Leveraging its inborn diversity for example, the priority of all the trans-European projects that the Commission co-finances for public and private institutions from all members state with the intention of fostering interaction among peoples form all countries. A very proactive way to bring together peoples from all the different cultures to develop projects, in all sectors, that capitalizes upon intelligence and inclusion, this contributes to sustaining the European Union leadership position in world markets.

Towards the nineties, scientists such as Offerman and Gowing (IPD, 1996) researched the impact of diversity in the corporate communities. The findings again confirmed that global mega-diversity, when managed, results in fostering innovation and therefore makes unprecedented contributions to the creation of mechanisms that are driving humanity to the highest levels of accelerated transformation.

IKEA is a great example of how the inclusion of diversity contributes to running a corporation with a high level of efficiency and sustainability. Ingvar

Kamprad—born in Småland, southern Sweden—at age five, sold matchboxes and had very set objective; he was going to be "the owner of a business." In 1940, at age seventeen he founded IKEA, a furniture design business. Now, IKEA not only sells furniture, but has joined UNICEF in defense of children, and cooperates with WWF to promote the use of alternative energy from its IKE suppliers. IKEA does not sell furniture; it offers a "do-it-yourself" philosophy that connects with the needs and preferences of a large part of the world population today. It offers the world population comfort, design, low prices and services, as well as a large number of home accessories, food, and the sense of belonging to a great movement, to a new way of living which society strongly demands. Kamprad was dyslexic, from one of the richest Scandinavian families. His fortune was estimated at 610 billion crowns, (65 billion euros). He was very efficiency-oriented as far as managing finances is concerned. IKEA owns 270 stores in forty-four countries around the world, which report sales of 20 billion euros and 120,000 employees of all profiles to connect with the different profiles of its 550 million customers that buy at IKEA every year. All its employees receive management focused training. Employees are responsible for the results of the space they manage and are trained to anticipate the needs of their customers. IKEA anticipated the need of distance workers and launched an office closet easy to fit small living quarters.

In 1999, the first Diversity Council in Europe was founded by the European delegation of The Conference Board, of which the European Institute for Diversity Management was one of the founding members, together with multinationals operating in Europe which already had diversity corporate policies in their organizations. Major corporations such as SHELL, Novartis, Cadbury Schweppes, British Telecom, Ikea, Sodexo, Deutsche Bank, and others were founding members. The European Institute for Managing Diversity was the only institution that was not a corporation. The council met four times a year, with the aim of exchanging experiences and benchmarking. Experts in the different subjects that interested the council members were invited to lecture and interact with the group. A very rich input. A Congress was organized every year open to public and private companies with prominent speakers from the European Union different directives as well as from the administrations where member companies of the Council presented best practices.

The European Diversity Council contributed, as the panel did in the United States in the eighties, to create and disseminate organizational policies to generate innovation and sustainable development. This was a major contribution to leverage the extremely profound diversity that has characterized the history of the peoples that have lived in the European continent. This mega diversity had never been leveraged as a positive factor for development, but rather has been a major source of conflicts—conflicts that had marked the history of the peoples that today make up the European Union space after signing the Treaty of Rome in 1957.

It was not until thirty years later, in 2008, that the first Diversity Council in Asia was created. It is interesting to appreciate the time it takes for decision makers of companies from different regions or continents to address new disciplines. In the case of Asia, the main reason for addressing diversity inclusion policies at that point was the high business exchange existing between US and EU companies with local organizations in Asia.

Yet in December 2021, Asia woke up and established a leading position regarding respect to diversity inclusion policies. The Association to Advance Collegiate of Schools of Business (AACSB), released a position paper that clearly articulates how they define diversity, equity, inclusion, and belonging (DEIB) and their unwavering commitment to advancing these principles around the world. "The manifesto keeps us grounded in our beliefs and unites us as we strive to ensure equitable access to high-quality business education around the world. We felt compelled to publish this paper to clearly express what we stand for given the diverse global communities we serve."

With this message, Jikyeong Kang, PhD, President, and Dean, MVP Chair in Marketing of the Asian Institute of Management, and member of the AACSB Board of Directors Chair, launched a movement to advance diversity in business education around the world.

For AACSB, diversity is a core value and is fundamental to fostering engagement, accelerating innovation, and amplifying impact in business education. Diversity in business can be achieved when business schools themselves embrace diversity within the communities they serve. Learners from a variety of backgrounds are inspired when they see role models and relatable examples represented in the faculty, staff, and curriculum, which fuels the pipeline for diverse leaders in business and society.

Jikyeong Kang, in describing the objective of AACSB states that of others "to establish diversity education within business schools worldwide, we must first define what we mean by diversity, equity, inclusion, and belonging to all our stakeholders, from faculty and learners to business leaders, organizations, and our own employees."

Diversity. AACSB defines diversity as culturally embedded identities rooted in historical and cultural traditions, legislative and regulatory concepts, ethnicity, gender, sexual orientation, socioeconomic conditions, religious practices, age, ability, and individual and shared experiences. When these differences are both recognized and respected through the delivery of high-quality business education, diversity becomes a powerful catalyst for unleashing the potential of an organization and individuals.

Equity. AACSB defines equity as providing access to high-quality business education globally. We recognize that, because we do not all share the same background, we have a responsibility to make sure that all individuals can grow, develop, and pursue their full potential through education.

Inclusion. AACSB defines inclusion as the opportunity for all individuals to participate. Inclusion requires that we empower people to respect and appreciate what makes us different.

Belonging. AACSB defines belonging as a feeling of safety, acceptance, and being valued in social, group, work, and community settings. Cultivating a sense of belonging on campus, online, and in the workplace is a fundamental part of creating a better workforce and society.

Statement of Jikyeong Kang for the Book

Corporations that manage diversity inclusion as a core policy frequently extend their policy to suppliers and client companies that share this inclusive polity and establish mechanisms to guarantee the respect for the different profiles of their workforce. A company does not start and end within its walls. Any business organization starts with its suppliers and ends when its clients have consumed the products or services of the company. Suppliers are a very valuable source of key information on new resources, new materials, new potential competitors that emerge. Extremely valuable information for the company to help anticipate change and future corporate sustainability in highly vulnerable and undertrain markets. When persons who have bought the product or service offered by the company "destroy" the product or service is when it is really consumed and when the company can project future sales and market positioning if it accurately analyses the indicators identified to measure the results. It is imperative to map the diversity profiles of the consumers in order to foster a diverse workforce which reflects that diverse map. That is when the corporate workforce makes a major contribution to the sustainability of the organization. Both suppliers and clients should be considered, treated, and included as preferred partners of the company.

As the Detroit Regional Chamber of Commerce states, inclusion of suppliers and clients to the corporate system could go back to the nineteen sixties when civil rights movements influenced the need to respect and include all types of differences of the population. By the eighties and nineties in the US diversity supplier was a common practice in the business community for social and economic reasons. A fluid relation with suppliers can represent high savings in logistics as well as a trustworthy source of innovation. This equally can apply to client inclusion. The loyalty and sense of belonging of clients is the result of matching the workforce profiles with that of its customers to establish a solid client base which is essential for the sustainability of any business.

In the U.K., supplier diversity legislation was first introduced in 2000 under the Local Government Act. This early directive outlined the responsibility that local authorities have to promote the social, economic, and environmental; well-being, of their communities through diverse procurement practices."

In France, similar legislation was adopted in 2006, Sweden followed suit by passing a public procurement act that prohibits discrimination based on nationality.

In 2014, the EU also passed a directive on the disclosure of nonfinancial and diversity information. This mandated corporate transparency has caused many EU companies to give more attention to issues such as sustainability, social and community impact, and diverse procurement practices. Germany and Spain still lag behind.

In the U.S., the majority of public sector supplier diversity programs are structured around legislative mandates instrumental in diversifying the national supply chain and encouraging businesses to build out their diverse supplier networks abroad including smaller business as well as those owned by minorities.

European nonprofit organizations have been instrumental in accelerating EU supplier diversity legislation and educating businesses to promote supplier diversity and economic inclusion in the global supply chain.

MBEs of the United States, like MUSDUK, EMBs and Center for Research in Ethnic Minority Entrepreneurship (CREME) on supplier diversity, immigration, and social inclusion helped influence corporate procurement policies and have since established a vast international network. Events are hosted for corporations to promote supplier diversity worldwide as a response to growing globalization. CREME gives recognition to Accenture, Price Waterhouse Cooper and Barclay´s Bank for excellence in supplier diversity inclusion.

This intercultural inclusive policy is key to the efficiency of the business process between companies. As business practices are carried out in diverse ways in the different countries, a constant awareness process must focus on understanding the cultural behavior of the people that conduct business in the other areas of the world where the companies operate. Understanding and respecting the times and work calendars of the other companies; being able to communicate in a common language; respect the management and communication styles of the personnel; all of these practices save money but above all, they created bridges that improve the results between both organizations. This is one more piece of evidence of the magnitude of diversities as an imperative need to manage in all kinds of alliances and business exchange worldwide.

CHAPTER 3

What is Diversity? Causes and Effects

The definitions given by the different institutions to the concept of "diversity" vary, as each organization addresses diversity from the perspective of its responsibility to the socio-economic environments. But in essence they all coincide in the universal need to take it into consideration in any decision-making process, whether of public or private institutions. Diversity is the essence of the nature of peoples and furthermore, it is an undeniable element in generating development in all fields of human behavior.

According to United Nations, "Diversity manifests itself in many ways. It is generally thought of in terms of demographic attributes: differences in age, race, gender, disability, sexual orientation, as well as in terms of cultural attributes, such as differences in religion, language, level of education, personal skills and abilities, or family structure. Diversity in terms of background takes as prevailing pattern: professional experience, specialization, lifestyle, values, culture, as well as social class."

Directive 2000 of the Directorate General V for Labor and Social Affairs of the Commission of the European Union in 2000, also proposed that Member States establish legislation to combat discrimination as a way of creating an environment of equal rights in the European Union: "The right that all citizens in the European Union have in access to work, promotion and salary, as well as to the conciliation of work and personal life, regardless their diverse profile of gender, race, ethnicity, age, disability, sexual orientation, culture, religion, as well as personal skills and abilities."

To contribute to this process, Directorate General V promoted the creation of the Diversity Charter to support the business community in its responsibility to promote diversity in the European Union to capitalize on its innate capacity to innovate. The definition of diversity with which the Charter was launched is as follows: "Managing diversity is therefore a corporate strategy focused on creating an inclusive environment that respects the right of access to work, promotion, compensation and work / family balance that all people regardless their diversities of gender, race, ethnicity, age, disability, sexual orientation, religion and other cultural profiles; as well as professional capacities and personal abilities. The aim is for companies to reduce costs and increase innovation and efficiency, as well as to contribute to profits and sustainability through fostering quality in work and life for all peoples."

When in 2011, Directorate General of Justice established the Directive to penalize discrimination on the basis of diversity profiles, diversity and inclusion management officially became a: a) social imperative, because it promotes the respect of people regardless their differences; b) an economic imperative, because it generates innovation and efficiency in organizations to contribute to their sustainable development; c) a legal imperative because discriminating on the bases of demographic or cultural difference is penalized by law in the European Union.

Kōichirō Matsuura, Director General of UNESCO between 1999 and 2009, delivered an outstanding speech on May 20th, 2005, on the occasion of the World Day for Cultural Diversity for Dialogue and Development, issuing a message that enshrines cultural diversity as common patrimony of humanity:

> I take this opportunity to express the need to respond to the challenges created by the current globalization processes which, while fostering a renewed dialogue between cultures and civilizations, highlights vulnerability of diversity.
>
> Cultural diversity has become fundamentally important for the future of societies to acquire new initiatives. Thus, the international community has entrusted UNESCO, which by virtue of its Constitution promotes the value diversity of the world's cultures, the task of drawing up a convention regarding the protection of diversity of cultural content and artistic expressions, particularly threatened by current processes that presently does not enjoy any special protection.
>
> For UNESCO, the need to work in this area is imperative, since cultural diversity defined as the result of the opening of cultures among themselves and its consequent exchanges, can only prosper if the conditions are met for each individual and each society to profit from its exceptional wealth.
>
> It involves guaranteeing each country and each social group, including persons belonging to minorities and indigenous groups, the possibility of participating in sustainable development.

The proclamation of principles established by UNESCO magnificently describes not only diversity, but also the affects it has on the work life of all humanity. In addition, it alerts the world population that diversity is an intrinsic factor of every person and, therefore, of all the activities they carry out. Diversity equally affects all peoples throughout the world and, in the same way, affects the companies as well as the public and private institutions that they create and manage in the different parts of the planet.

Readers can find the entire content of the Declaration in the Annex of the book. It is extremely useful to read as it clears any doubt about the value that diversity has had, has and will have in the life and activities of humanity.

The Royal European Academy of Doctors, in the person of its president, Alfredo Rocafort Nicolau, invited the academic world to include Diversity in its curriculum research activities in order to promote the development of subjects that provide the necessary educational content regarding the management of diversity inclusion in training centers, as well as in postgraduate projects. This is an extraordinary and essential step to advance the education of decision makers, as well as the entire workforce of public and private institutions in the creation of innovation and efficiency, fundamental to achieving sustainable organizations in scenarios with growing speed of transformation.

> From the Royal European Academy of Doctors (RAED) we recognize the importance of diversity in society. Therefore, from the academic world we want to promote research on the application of inclusion policies in all types of organizations. Analyzing the challenges, assessing the advantages and disseminating the results will be the way to succeed in having enterprises institutions bet on diversity as a key competitive strategy.

There is no doubt that the processes of inclusion of differences generate initiatives and developments that constantly transform the scenarios. It is a continuous and systemic feedback process. Humanity (men and women) transform the world from the micro to the macro, as long as the value of the inclusion of the differences that identifies them is promoted as a value and not as a menace. Just as water is made up by the combination of two gas elements, men and women with their multiple differences come together to form humanity. In this sense, Bruce Lee gave us a life lesson with his famous phrase, "be water my friend," inspired by Chinese philosophy. The sustainable process is therefore based on men and women building on their complexity in social as well as professional arenas. Operating then from their complementarity as a single entity without friction or requirement; each contributing with their own and diverse skills and abilities.

This explains, for instance, the different ways in which companies develop and how their results depend on the capacity for dialogue, interpersonal relationships, fluent and effective communication between all their peoples to build upon the contribution they can each make based on their diverse profiles and different innovative, ethical and leadership capabilities.

Amancio Ortega, founder of ZARA (Inditex), created a network of fashion stores that sell fashion and accessories with an extremely efficient worldwide distribution. This is a company which in 2020 had 7,000 stores in 202 different countries. On the other hand, Ramón Areces and César Rodríguez (from Cuba) founded El Corte Inglés on June 28, 1940, a network of fashion and accessories stores with 174 outlets exclusively in the Spanish market. Both organizations have been extremely successful, as both have built on their differences to position themselves in their respective markets. The coronavirus pandemic represents a great sustainability challenge for their respective business structures, which they will of course manage in very different ways. Inditex faces the transformation of 202 different social, economic, political, and legislative environments, while El Corte Inglés must manage a single social and economic environment. The strategic solutions that each of the companies will implement will be very different and respond to their very diverse business purpose.

In March 2006, Gonzalo Sánchez Gardey PhD, Vice-Dean of the University of Cádiz, published his cum laude thesis, "Strategic management of human resources and diversity in work groups: a structural analysis of moderating effects." The thesis was evaluated at an European level and establishes a milestone in the scientific study of diversity as a critical factor in this new era.

The fundamental factor of group and teamwork in the development of innovation and efficiency is clearly established. The thesis conclusion is that the models of strategic management of human resources and that of the diversity profiles of its workforce are complementary, for which he provides a management model that allows him to systematically define management patterns to leverage and moderate the different effects of demographic and psychosocial heterogeneity of groups. Innovation is the result of inclusive group work.

CHAPTER 4

Dynamics of Change: Exponential in Times of Discontinuity

The reality of diversity at a global and local level is appreciated from the impulse given by two engines and two trends that transform present and future scenarios in continuous transformation.

The speed of change is increasingly accelerated, which is an advantage for the development of innovations, but also represents a cost for companies, which must continually update the knowledge and competence of their teams to be able to put new products into practice and systems that become part of the tools of daily use. To appreciate this reality, it is enough to review the period of time that an invention or innovation has taken to emerge, imposing a discontinuity with respect to the above.

Reaching the steam propulsion engine developed by Robert Fulton in the United States took 178 years, while it only took three years to go from the gasoline engine, created by the German Nicolaus Otto or twenty years for the electric motor. This rhythm opens up opportunities for the development of alternative energies that contribute to environmental care.

It took ninety-four years to go from ultraviolet radiation invented by the German Johann Wilhelm in 1801 to x-rays, discovered in 1895 by the also German Wilhelm Conrad Röntgen. And only five years to go to gamma rays in 1900, at the hands of the French Paul Ulrich Villard, a step that made technology the great ally for early diagnosis. On average, about 1,479 new applications appear every day; in fact, Google alone has released more than 20,000, in addition to 52,000 registered patents.

The effects of the speed of change are evident in all sectors and human activities, with the aggravating factor that its impact may vary in different parts of the world due to the different capacities of each people to accept, understand, and use these changes. The agents of the various scenarios change and transform continuously, some in unsuspected directions, but, innovation, people take it as their own.

The power of computers doubles every twelve months, which is a very high replacement cost for any organization, to which is added the need for training, updating the skills of its people, the incorporation of new talents, and the consequent loss of workers who do not have the necessary skills. This factor is not always measured and valued economically and humanely.

The average life of the products is three months, which means that when the first euro is earned with the new product, it is already obsolete. Market acceptance, in turn, encourages other people or companies to identify a business opportunity. Each company must create its own discontinuity before competitors do, incorporating innovation that allows it to maintain dominance over the markets. The company cannot lose so much ground that price is its differential factor, because its days will be numbered and when it wants to react, it will no longer have funds to finance its repositioning. For this reason, the iPhone replaces itself every year.

And it is that businesses for life or long-term products that no longer exist. Business management must manage the speed of replacement and the discontinuity of all types of technologies, products, and services that come onto the market; users are diverse, as are regions, countries, and cultures that demand that their needs be met to continually update their lifestyle. To achieve this constant repositioning, the company must have a workforce that reflects the profiles of its consumers in order to connect with its audiences effectively. Communications technology shrinks the world and turns everyone into neighbors, as well as organizations, which as a result become equally diverse.

Google receives 600 million requests for information a day. There is no doubt that both Larry Page and Sergei Brin, aged twenty-nine and thirty have changed the world by founding Google on September 24, 1998.

Facebook was created by Mark Zuckerberg in 2004 and, within one year, it reached eleven million users. His goal was that his classmates at Harvard University could be in contact and facilitate communication between young students. Years later, Facebook became the vehicle Egyptians used to call for unprecedented mass demonstrations that were ultimately key to overthrowing Mubarak. On August 24, 2015, one in seven inhabitants of the world agreed on Facebook.

Jack Dorsey founded Twitter on March 21, 2006, when the first tweet was posted. Today, it is a perfect sociological x--ray that works through 280 characters and is visited by one in fourteen people in the world who seek to converse, comment, and create bonds of friendship. Donald Trump, during his presidency of the United States, used Twitter as a political platform to announce the policies and strategies of his administration on a daily basis. Arguably, it paved the way for world leaders to turn to Twitter to personally communicate with their citizens.

Every second, the inhabitants of this planet get closer to each other thanks to the use they give to the big social networks: Google receives 3.8 million searches; Instagram publishes 65,000 photos; Facebook uploads 243,000 photos; Netflix makes 87,000 videos available; more than 1.5 million songs are listened to on Spotify; YouTube incorporates 400 hours of video; WhatsApp allows the sending of 29 million messages, surpassing the use of landlines in developed countries; Scape makes more than 2 million calls per minute and 56,000 emails are sent per second; LinkedIn, the largest network of professionals in the world with 575 million users, increases by 120 new accounts per second; Globalization arises from the ability to reach all parts of the world in real time and to be able to maintain communication and interact socially and professionally with people from very different regions, with diverse cultures and governance systems.

If anyone doubts the effect of globalization, one only has to remember the impact that COVID-19 has on the entire world population, which began to spread between December 12 and 29 in the Chinese city of Wuhan. There were governments that began to take measures to protect their citizens in January, but others also acted slower, perhaps thinking that it would not come, so the population has paid the consequences. And, in fact, the seven countries with a woman as head of government are the ones that have best managed the start of the epidemic. Again, the power of diversity. Angela Merkel in Germany, Jacinda Ardern in New Zealand, Tsai Ing-wen in Thailand, Vigdís Finnbogadóttir in Iceland, Sanna Marin in Finland, Erna Solberg in Norway, and Mette Frederiksen in Denmark.

These seven women leaders achieved excellent management thanks to common factors, such as quick and executive decision-making capacity, effective, clear, empathetic messages, maximum creativity, and less margin for error. They started faster and with the conviction that this way they would better endure the future. Instead, Donald Trump in the United States ignored the effect of the virus, and the country was ranked 94th out of 100 in a Lowy Institute ranking. Pedro Sánchez's Spain was ranked 78th and the United Kingdom, under Boris Johnson, 95th, denied the existence of the danger of contagion until he himself became infected. Colombia, Mexico, and Brazil occupied the last positions. As a result, the virus spread rapidly throughout the world, and only when there were already local infections, did these countries begin to take sanitary measures to combat such a dangerous disease for humanity.

However, the COVID-19 pandemic has brought very positive transformations, at least to developed countries. In August 2020, fifty fewer people died in Spain than in August 2019. The same has happened in Sweden. The reason is that people have learned to value and take better care of their health, and to take fewer unnecessary risks, a behavior that will last beyond the pandemic.

Companies have learned that telecommuting is much more efficient and profitable for the organization, as it is for workers of all ranks except the assembly line, but these will be replaced by robots. People who work remotely manage their time and can reconcile their professional functions with their personal and family needs. This is a social advance of a gigantic scope that is going to affect our lives in many ways: the services that people who work in person need for their homes, such as care for the family or children; the type of supply for the home, redefining which products and services will be in demand and which ones will have to rethink their offer; the retail sector, which loses business volume if it is maintained only in person; and large companies, such as Zara, Galeries Lafayette, Bloomingdale's, which must reinvent the management of their infrastructures; and to all suppliers in this and other sectors. Humanity is entering a new era.

The offer of leisure, sports, training and culture will change. And companies will be more efficient thanks to a greater performance of their people and the enormous savings in infrastructure, by not having to house their total payroll in office spaces, which, among other things, will redefine the real estate sector. They will have to build houses with workspace for those who inhabit them.

Work for third parties will be the scarcest good. It will be necessary to move towards new forms of work as a habitual norm: distance work, part-time, shared work and a four-day week, an increase in the number of freelancers and entrepreneurs, etc. Work must be measured by the fulfillment of the functions that are performed and not by the time of presence of the people, because the working hours—the hours of hiring of a person—do not guarantee the effective performance of the work. In fact, for this reason, Spain has come to occupy the 49th place in efficiency in the world ranking. It is crucial to launch a total transformation of the business, social, cultural, and political world with a view to a higher quality of life.

The long-awaited birth rate in developed countries will increase, as couples will be able to take care of their children thanks to remote work, which is already the preferred mode of work. Seventy-two percent of the employees who work remotely since the pandemic began want to continue with this type of work. Hotels like Coral Hotels de Canarias are being reconverted to offer attractive, comfortable, and efficient places to live and work for people who do not have to be present in the office or even in the country. And so, a new way of life arises that harmonizes work, personal life, and leisure in an attractive way, creating new offers of products and services by sectors such as real estate, tourism, restaurants, and fashion.

The entrepreneurial world will open multiple opportunities and offers to different sectors of the workforce, since people will have more time to devote to personal activities. To start an entrepreneurial or business activity, the question is: what needs do different sectors of the population have to occupy their personal, family, and leisure time? Those are the new businesses and professional activities that are going to be developed successfully. There will be no small or large companies, but small or large implementations of ideas and initiatives. Uber, a company that offers car service with a driver, could have chosen to be a local company, but preferred to grow and is today one of the largest global companies. Any type of service company will be able to choose its size in the future, adapting to the people who start it up and know how to anticipate the needs of increasingly diverse audiences.

And it is that as globalization has brought people of all profiles closer together, it has awakened the evidence of the diversities that emerge in the world. Also, it has become aware that this diversity is part of the lives of all the inhabitants of the planet and, therefore, of its manifestations —organizations, entities and companies which build technologies to contribute to improving the quality of life of people and, in principle, serve society. Globalization has and will have a strong impact on the different governance systems that govern different areas of the world, of everything that people do and create.

As an example, ABB, a Swiss multinational corporation based in Zurich, is a world leader in electrical power generation, industrial automation, and robotics technologies, operating in more than one hundred countries and employing more than 145.000 people. The development in intercultural competence of its people is one of the five axes of its corporate policy. Of the same way businessmen and women have to understand that their potential domestic market is made up of the entire world population and that this target population is infinitely diverse. Therefore, organizations must have workers whose profiles reflect the cultural differences, whether in language, lifestyle, preferences, or needs of all the countries where they operate. The workforce has to be diverse in order to maintain a sustainable positioning in the markets in which it operates. The effectiveness of the organization depends on the matching of employee profiles with those of the organization's customers and suppliers. All the inhabitants of the planet depend to a greater or lesser extent on products and services from other parts of the world for their daily lives.

Amazon (USA) generates 61 billion dollars in sales worldwide, since purchases made on the virtual platform have gone from 100 million to 250 million in four years. The challenge for Amazon is in the physical delivery of products due to the logistical complexity in different locations on the planet, especially in rural areas where drones can play a very important role.

On the other hand, Alibaba Group (阿里巴巴 集团) is a private Chinese consortium based in Hangzhou founded in 1999 by Chinese businessman Jack Ma. It functions as a business-to-business site, to connect Chinese manufacturers with buyers from all over the world and, in fact, it houses the Taobao portal for consumer-to-consumer sales that competes with eBay and that today has more than 1000 products and is responsible for 60% of the packages that are delivered in China. In 2010, AliExpress was founded, business-to-consumer, a low-cost platform that directly connects Chinese manufacturers with customers globally. Alibaba brought in 376,844 million yuan (48,981 million euros) in 2018, an improvement of 51% over the previous year. With more than 22,000 employees and 654 million users, it is larger than eBay and Amazon combined.

In 2019, the world came to a standstill with the pandemic. Humanity and its institutions will be reinvented. Therefore, it is compulsory for future leaders to acquire new skills and abilities to address new scenarios. This is the philosophy that governs the teaching system of Ubiquity University, founded by Jim Garrison, with the aim of training leaders for future scenarios.

Because it is essential that today's future executives, entrepreneurs, politicians and leaders can develop the knowledge, competencies, and skills that allow them to seize the opportunities that new changing environments will bring to humanity in the future, Jim Garrison has founded the University Ubiquity (www.ubiquityuniversity.org), an accredited academic institution operating as a California-based technology and education platform institution. Based on the belief that people everywhere must be supported with the social skills and professional competencies they need to solve urgent global problems that threaten planetary ecology and human society. The University offers competency-based face-to-face and virtual learning experiences to earn

BA, MA, MBA and Ph.D. accreditations, certificates, and degrees. The programs are designed for social agents of change and entrepreneurs of all kinds, who are destined to transform personal passion into collaborative actions for the common good. With a solid financial backing, Ubiquity University offers educational products in the global market and the construction of a Global Database that links skills, talent, and training accessed through an Artificial Intelligence program.

Because humanity will never go back to where it was, Jim Garrison invites all forward minded people to participate in the Humanity Rising Leadership Summit to redesign the way everyone will live and move forward from here to a world more sustainable and healthier, taking advantage of the fact that there is now a crack in the global system.

> Humanity Rising is an initiative of Ubiquity University and over 350 partnering organizations worldwide to create a daily global commons on Zoom from 8:00 - 9:30 AM PST Monday through Friday to enable people globally to come together to share their experiences as we all navigate through the pandemic and take counsel together as to how we can increase our strategic effectiveness. We held our first broadcast on May 22, 2020, and now broadcast over live streaming partner channels to about 15,000 - 20,000 people each day, although for designated programs we create "waves" which enable us to go out to several hundred thousand. We've had over 1,500 speakers. During COP 26, we had a twelve-day program which included activists from Glasgow and globally that we estimate reached seven to ten million. We cover a range of issues, but the meta theme has from the beginning been the pandemic.
>
> What has been most important for Humanity Rising are the partnerships that have arisen. Three important coalitions that have emerged from Humanity Rising are the Masters in Regenerative Action, the Global Accreditation Council, and the Global Regeneration Corps. The only way for the progressive movement to make a significant difference is through Radical Collaboration; turning conversations that matter into actions that make a difference.

Participants are invited to give a presentation for the Summit on a topic of their choice that is most important to them with the aim of building a better world, given their personal experience to lead a creative discussion and working group. Sessions are virtual and are announced in the weekly Summit report for members to join those of their specific interest.

The world came to a standstill, most people have some kind of lockdown to overcome. Over the coming months and years, different countries will experience the implementation of different strategies to overcome this crisis. The key is to create leaders with anticipated vision to identify opportunities and lead people to achieve renewed objectives with high degree of confidence, success and sustainability.

Humanity Rising is an initiative of Ubiquity University with over 350 partnering organizations worldwide to create a daily global commons on Zoom from 8:00 - 9:30 AM PST Monday through Friday to enable people globally to come together to share their experiences as we all navigate through the pandemic and take counsel together as to how we can increase our strategic effectiveness. We held our first broadcast on May 22, 2020 and now broadcast over live streaming partner channels to about 15,000 - 20,000 people each day, although for designated programs we create "waves" which enable us to go out to several hundred thousand. We've had over 1,500 speakers. During COP 26, we had a twelve-day program which included activists from Glasgow and globally that we estimate reached seven to ten million. We cover a range of issues, but the meta theme has from the beginning been the pandemic.

What has been most important for Humanity Rising are the partnerships that have arisen. Three important coalitions that have emerged from Humanity Rising are the Masters in Regenerative Action, the Global Accreditation Council, and the Global Regeneration Corps. The only way for the progressive movement to make a significant difference is through Radical Collaboration: Turning conversations that matter into actions that make a difference.

The forefront plan for the 2020 Summit was to be involved and contributing as world events unfold. It is clear that this virus is not going to disappear suddenly. The Summit wanted to be present in this catharsis and so holds important process with daily blogs, virtual debates, and most importantly, propose creative solutions. The goal is to redesign the future in which humanity can live a healthy and sustainable existence.

The Humanity Rising Global Solutions Summit launched on May 22, 2020. At that time, Humanity Rising represented a growing movement of people and organizations coming together to take counsel on how we can leverage the crisis of the COVID-19 pandemic into an opportunity for human renewal and increased resilience to future challenges.

Since that time, Humanity Rising has held over 330 daily sessions on a range of topics from politics, ecology, science, spirituality, and culture with over 20,000—30,000 people tuning in from various streaming platforms each day. Speakers that have participated in the Summit include over 1300 distinguished individuals.

One year later, Ubiquity President and Founder Dr. Jim Garrison, who hosts every session of Humanity Rising, reflects on the past eighteen months: "After over 300 sessions, we are seeing the power of radical collaboration. Out of Humanity Rising has emerged a coalition of groups that have come together to establish a whole new kind of MBA a Masters in Regenerative Action. The Humanity Rising collaboration has also given rise to the Global Regeneration Corps, which is activating pods of Regeneration First Responders globally. The power of radical collaboration is key to human survival in a time of Code Red for our climate emergency.

Each day, the Summit convene for two hours from 8:00 to 10:00 AM PDT at 5:00—7:00 PM CET to engage in presentations, group dialogues and working groups. The Summit will continue for as long as the pandemic lasts. It will feature daily TED Talks-style presentations from influential figures such as Jane Goodall, Charles Eisenstein, and Vandana Shiva, as well interactive sessions with leaders from international organizations such as Synergos, Impact HUBS, Regenerate Costa Rica, Gaia Education, Humanity's Team, Ideanco, Masterpeace, Age Nation, Pachamama Alliance, Global Ecovillage Network,Crowdsourcing Week, Heart Ambassadors, Davos Blockbase, and many more. Individuals and organizations are welcome to play a part in the Summit as speakers, panelists, contributors, or participants.[1]

---

1. For more information about registration, participation, speakers, events, and more, please visit: www.humanityrising.solutions or contact r.jayasinghe@ubiquityuniversity.org with any queries.

CHAPTER 5

A New Socio-economy:
Diverse Ways of Financing Business

Business Angels are a fundamental actor in the innovation ecosystem, being the first private investors that typically support brand new *startup businesses at a moment where risk of failure of these ventures is extremely high. By providing crucial strategic support, mentorship*, and connections, in addition to capital to the startups they invest in, business angels enable entrepreneurs in launching and growing businesses, contributing therefore to the advancement of technological progress, economic growth, job creation and societal wellbeing.

Research from Harvard Business School's Prof. Josh Lerner shows that startups that have an angel investor among their shareholders are much more likely to survive their first years of trading and create more jobs: "Start-ups funded by angel investors are 14%-23% more likely to survive for the next 1.5 to 3 years and grow their employment by 40% relative to non-angel-funded start-ups."

Over 7B Euros are invested every year on the European continent alone by angel investors, with over 35,000 new startups each year receiving financial and strategic support from such investors. Approximately two thirds of all private investment in "pre-seed" and "seed" *stages (in Europe; approximately* 11B Euros in 2020) is performed solely by business angels.

EBAN (www.eban.org), the European Business Angels Network and the trade association representing the angel investment community across Europe since 1999 promotes and spreads the culture of angel investment on the European continent by enabling network connections, best practice sharing, and cross border syndication support to over one hundred angel groups and 3000 business angels across 50+ countries. EBAN strives to create a European nation of investors that is knowledgeable and professional in supporting the next generation of startup entrepreneurs.

Without angel investors, many of the tech companies we know about today would not be here. Without business angels, the later stage investment community such as VCs and Private Equity, would not have the same access as they do nowadays to quality high growth opportunities to invest in. Business angels are key to the success of any startup community and their activities must be fostered by both private and public stakeholders.

Jacopo Losso
Director European Association of Business Angels

In 1970, 84M persons in the world migrated. Yet the United Nations global estimate is that 281M persons migrated in 2020, representing 3.6% of the world population. Migration movement is driven by structural factors in their countries in search of jobs that would allow them to survive; in spite of the challenge of language differences as well as of cultural and political diversities that conditions life and work.

Walter Acitis Miguel Angel de Prada y Carlos Pereda (Colectivo Joe) carried out in 1993 very premonitory research to evaluate the global population mobility. The findings showed that already at that time 1.7% of the world population migrated mainly from underdeveloped countries in search of work. The main reason at that time that compelled people to leave their countries was to find jobs that gave them a salary to live and to send back to their families for their survival.

Whereas in the seventies the majority of emigrants were clerical, service workers, and domestic, basically hand labor, by the nineties, the profiles of the migrant population was one of high education levels.

In 1920, United Nations certified that 2.8% of the world population had migrated, and in 2020, the International Labor Organization reported that 3.6% of the global population migrated to other parts of the world making "brain drain" a major challenge for regions and nations in their need of sustainable development in times when talent is a major asset of any organization, company, country, or region. Talent mobility in Europe has tripled in the past fifteen years while in China and the United States it has doubled.

While the North of Europe attracts talent, the south is impoverished in terms of human and labor capital. In 2021, Spain was first on the list, losing 2.5M highly qualified workers (university or higher degree) followed by Italy and Greece

India is by far the country with the highest number of migrant workers of all types of profiles. South American countries hold historical workers' migration to Spain and Portugal because of the close intercultural links.

First in the list of countries attracting talent is the United States followed by several European countries such as the United Kingdom, Germany, Switzerland, Netherlands, Sweden, and France are leading in attracting highly qualified young students and professionals in information technology, research, finances, and new competences that go from inter-culturality, social skills to artificial intelligence.

The research highlights three main motivations when crossing borders: salaries, the lack of demand from business, and life satisfaction: that is, the quality of institutions, public services, lifestyle, etc.

"The World Economic Forum launched in January 2020 is working with over 350 organizations to provide 1 billion people with better education, skills and economic opportunities by 2030. 1.1 billion jobs are liable to be radically transformed by technology and growing diverse social behavior in the next decade. This ambitious programme that will benefit 100 million people around the world is preparing the global workforce with the skills needed to develop their carriers in the future, as technologies such as artificial intelligence enable greater automation."

Belonging

In this new scenario, countries, regions, and the business community must re-think its ways of retaining talent of the young generation in which local institutions have invested. The objective is to create organizations that attract people to its workforce in order to achieve efficiency and leverage constant innovation that will guarantee corporate sustainability in environments in profound transformation.

Persons do not comply any longer with performing any type of function in an organization for eight or ten hours of their lives, just to earn a salary that covers their living expenses. More and more individuals today and in the future value their time as their key asset and want to dedicate it to those activities that they like, enjoy, and above all feel that they are a part of. Belonging, being part og the project, then becomes a core factor and then determines the quality of working life and the impact of their contribution to corporate bottom line. Sustainability is then the result as people are treated as partners of the organization and equally share its objective. Very powerful policy.

Another result of personal time management is a crucial aspect of work that is being pushed increasingly to the forefront of organization design: self-selection-based division of labor. Essentially the process of matching workers with tasks, division of labor in organizations was, until recently, a top-down allocation exercise presided over by managers. Presently and towards the future workers are increasingly empowered to assign tasks to themselves a result of high talent development.

At the software firm Valve and French auto parts maker FAVI, for example, employees select tasks as well as project teams based on their own perceptions of best fit. In fact, at many software firms and other less hierarchical organizations, self-selection has become the norm for its positive effect on employee motivation.

Although task allocation remains dominant and continues to flourish even in innovation-intensive sectors, Massimo Warglien states that "self-selection would outperform the managerial allocation of tasks even if there were no motivational benefits: when employees are highly specialized, the tasks are independent of each other, and employee availability is unforeseeable and employee belonging to the project becomes a major asset to the organization."

At Burtzorg, procedures were explicitly designed to share unpopular administrative chores equitably among nurses. Another way to prevent tasks from going unstaffed is to encourage employees to pick those to which they could add the most value or make the most difference, rather than to choose those in which they are most skilled.

Seven out of ten persons in the world are self-employed. Looking at the global state of self-employment, it becomes apparent that there is in fact an inverse correlation between the proportion of self-employed workers and the GDP of their countries. According to data from the International Labor Organization, only 12.2 percent of workers are self-employed on average in high-income economies while in low-income economies, this figure rises to 80.3 percent. This is an indicator of the prevalence of subsistence farming and people working without pay for their family businesses (also counted as self-employed in the data).

Figures speak for themselves: 95.10 percent of the population in Niger, 95.8 percent in India, and 63.7 percent in Senegal are self-employed. It is interesting to find that 44.7 percent of the working population in China do not depend upon jobs created by the industrialized sector of the giant while in Colombia there is 49.69 percent of the population self-employed. Japan with a 10.1 percent and the United States, with 9.548M self-employed, are 6.8%

down in the UBL ranking. Closing the list are Kuwait and Qatar, this number was even lower at 1.8 percent and 0.4 percent, respectively.

This is growing trend. According to FreshBooks survey 96 percent of Americans that work for themselves have no desire to return to a regular job. Many self-employed professionals say that working for themselves provides a liberating opportunity to change their career. However, many individuals choose to work in the same field with the same clients or of the company they used to work for.

New Business Explosion

More significant is the need of people to manage their own time, lives, and work as revealed by the latest Mastercard's Recovery Insight: Small Business Reset report which corroborates this development, revealing a pandemic small-business boom. According to the report, "thirty-two percent more SMBs were set up in 2020 globally, as pent-up savings, a disrupted job market, and evolving consumer behaviors drove new entrepreneurship. From the UK and Canada to Japan and Brazil, countries around the world saw unprecedented new business formation growth, with the top 10 seeing a nearly 30% increase or more. The global economic marketplace rarely reacts in such unison, particularly as a result of crises. Yet this growth demonstrates that a lesser-known outcome from the past 18 months has been the innovation born from this worldwide disruption, as a host of new digitally native businesses were created to meet evolving needs, new market opportunities and a global shift to remote-work environments, which has enabled the entrepreneurial movement to thrive."

The top ten countries with the largest new business formation growth in 2020 were the UK (+101%), US (+86%), Australia (+73%), Germany (+62%) and Canada (+58%). Italy (+44%), France (+40%), Japan (+38%), Brazil (+35%), and Thailand (+29%). The numbers released by the U.S. Census Bureau, found a whopping 5.4M new business applications filed in 2021, surpassing the record set in 2020 of 4.4 million.

The pandemic has triggered innovation and created a host of new digitally native businesses designed to meet evolving needs and new market opportunities, specifically Market opportunities for people that want to manage their own time and life, doing what they like best doing, what they belong to and feel a part of. Emerging market opportunities for the creation of new services and products to meet the growing diverse needs, tastes and profiles of the global population.

In the European Union 99% of enterprises are small and middle-sized companies with under 250 employees that are responsible for the creation 85% of the workplace Small and medium-sized enterprises (SMEs) are a focal point in shaping business policy in the European Union (EU). The European Commission considers SMEs and entrepreneurship key to guarantee economic growth, innovation, job creation, and social integration in the EU.

The fully-fledged European Innovation Council (EIC), launched in March 2021 under Horizon Europe, is a major new player in the innovation landscape.

Its unique approach to identifying, developing, and scaling up Europe's breakthrough technologies and game-changing innovation is already delivering tangible results.

During its pilot phase, the EIC supported 5500 start-ups and SMEs which have crowded in EUR 9.6 billion in follow on investments, reached a valuation of around EUR 50 billion, and an increasing number of women-led start-ups; of those awarded funding in 2020, over 20 percent have a female CEO, a doubling of the previous level.

The start-ups trend is the growing choice of people to set up their own business and has created very diverse financing systems that emerge as an alternative to traditional banking loans. Start-up innovators not only need the capital to fund their ideas, but they also need partnership in sharing these ideas and developing a sustainable business project.

Seed capital is a first choice. It is an early investment. This means that the business is supported in its creation phase to pilot the idea until it manages to generate its own cash flow, or until it is ready for a real type and volume of investment which the business project needs to expand. Seed capital can include options such as family and friend financing, or any type of personal fundraising.

A local alternative is that of Community Development Finance which is available in most countries by state institutions, which have programs to finance local business projects.

Sporzynski, a US lending organization said, "A wide variety of applications for loans come across our desk every week, many of them from ambitious start-ups. As a mission-oriented non-bank lender, we know from experience that many viable small businesses struggle to access the capital they need to get started, thrive and grow."

CDFI lenders look at credit scores, too, but in a different way from banks in order to evaluate the person behind the project that requires financing.

"We look for borrowers who have been fiscally responsible, but we understand that unfortunate things happen to good people and businesses," Sporzynski said. "We seek to understand what happened and assess its relevance."

Bank loans are the traditional way to finance personal and professional projects. As of the third quarter of 2021, the total value of funding in banking start-ups worldwide reached a peak of 20.4 US dollars. A considerable increase over the 11.6 billion US dollars in 2020. Nevertheless, capital from traditional banks is difficult for small businesses to access for several reasons. Banks are not in the business of financing ideas; they are in the business of investing the deposits of their clients in operations that give them a high return in order to reward their shareholders. Banks have an outdated, labor-intensive lending process and regulations that are unfavorable to new entrepreneurs and small organizations. The difficulty of accessing capital is exacerbated because many small businesses applying for loans are new, and banks typically want to see at least a five-year profile of a healthy business (for instance, five years of tax data) before extending an offer.

There is a growing scope of options for startups and business development. Most businesses start small. And there are several reasons why entrepreneurs might turn to business loan alternatives. The four most common reasons are: lower credit requirements, easier qualification, faster approval, and ongoing partnership support.

Alternative Financing

Serkes believes that "with diverse alternative loans, a business owner gets a strong, invested partner who can introduce them to new clients, analysts, media and other contacts. Startups can therefore enjoy a few key benefits in securing funding from a nontraditional source."

Grants from different government or private foundations as well as Crowd funding on platforms such as Kickstarter and Indiegogo can give a financial boost to people looking to set up their own small businesses.

"As an entrepreneur, you don't want to spend your investment options and increase the risk of investing in your business at such an early age," said Igor Mitic, co-founder of Fortunly. "By using crowdfunding, you can raise the necessary seed funds to get your startup through the first stage of the project."

In the United States, there is variety of options to respond to the growing need people have to manage their own professional schemes, free from depending on a job that takes a large part of their time and personal freedom. Convertible debt is when a business borrows money from an investor or investor group and the collective agreement is to convert the debt to equity in the future. A merchant cash advance is the opposite of a small business loan in terms of affordability and structure. Microloans (or micro financing) are small loans given to entrepreneurs who have little to no collateral. In invoice financing, also known as factoring, a service provider fronts the money on the outstanding accounts receivable, which is repaid once customers settle their bills.

Venture Capital

Venture capitalism (VCs) is a worldwide business in itself. US Venture Capitalists' investments in 2021 doubled that of 2020. And 2022 was expected to end with over $612 billion in venture capital activity, a 108 percent increase from the year before. Generally, groups of investors get together willing to invest in an idea and take part ownership of the company they finance in exchange for capital which is negotiated in each case beforehand. Besides financing the project, the start-up entrepreneurs incorporate the experience and relationships of the VC group. A very valuable asset for the efficient development and sustainability of the business idea towards future growth.

"A lot of entrepreneurs lack the skills needed to grow a business, and even though they can make money through sales, understanding how to grow a company will always be a lost cause in the beginning," said Chris Holder, author of Tips to Success and CEO and founder of the $100 Million Run Group. "The guidance from an experienced investor group is the best thing, as the mentorship is key for everyone."

Business Angels

The term "business angels" investors has its origin in Broadway plays from the beginning of the 20th century. Those who financed these works were referred to as "angels."

"Groups, networks and the business angels' investment process," is a research project conducted by Stefano Bonini, Stevens Institute of Technology School of Business USA, Vincenzo Capizzi, Department of Economics and Business Studies, Università del Piemonte, Mario Valletta, Department of Economics and Business Studies, Università del Piemonte Orientale, and Paola Zocchi, Department of Economics and Business Studies, Università del Piemonte, Italy. A thorough report that projects the role of business angels in present and future development of business models of socio-economic growth. Such a role responds to the changing diverse profiles of people who want to establish their own professional environment and be masters of their own time. This represents a move. A way from traditional banking and loan strategies towards partnership development between the idea creators and the financers of these project to jointly create sustainable organizations.

In the last few years, both academics and practitioners have devoted increased attention to understanding the dynamics of business angel (BA) investments. Market data for both the US and Europe (US ACA, 2015; EVCA, 2014; EBAN, 2015; KraemerEis et al., 2015; OECD, 2016) show that business angels have become a major segment of the capital market industry, capable of allocating financial resources to one of the riskiest asset classes —startup companies— comparable to those historically provided by professional venture capitalists.

Angel capital fills the gap, in financing a start-up business, between the seed capital-founder-family-friends sources of capital, and institutional investors such as venture capital entities funds. Accessible family and friends' capital generally does not exceed $100,000 to finance the business idea, while most venture capital firms won't consider investments of less than $1M depending on the sector and country to invest in.

Jeffrey Sohl, director of the UNH Center for Venture Research, reports that the angel investor market in 2020 saw an increase in both the number of active investors and the number of investments as well as a six percent increase in the total dollars invested by angels, according to the latest angel market analysis by the Center for Venture Research at the University of New Hampshire. For the first time in several years, the seed and start-up stage market became the predominant investment stage for angels.

Total angel investments in 2020 were $25.3 billion, an increase of six percent over 2019. A total of 64,480 entrepreneurial ventures received angel funding, an increase of 1.2 percent over 2019 investments. The number of active investors also increased to 334,680 as compared to 323,365 in 2019, an increase of 3.5 percent.

In addition, angel investments in the seed and start-up stage were thirty-nine percent in 2020, and investments in early-stage investing was thirty-two percent in 2020, down from forty-six percent in 2019.

"For the first time in several years the seed and start-up stage market became the predominant investment stage, solidifying the trend in increasing allocations to seed and start-up ventures that began in 2018 at the expense of early-stage investing," said Jeffrey Sohl, director of the UNH Center for Venture Research. "With angels as the leading source of seed and start-up capital, this increase is encouraging for entrepreneurs."

The average angel deal size in 2020 was $392,025, an increase of 4.8 percent from 2019. The average equity received was 9.6 percent with a deal valuation of $4.1 million, a slight increase from 2019. "Valuation trends are likely an indication of upward pressure on valuations resulting in overvaluations in some sectors and/or regions of the angel market," said Sohl.

The Center for Venture Research has been conducting research on the angel market since 1980. The center's mission is to provide an understanding of the angel market through quality research. It provides reliable and timely information on the angel market to entrepreneurs, private investors, and public policymakers.

The University of New Hampshire inspires innovation and transforms lives in the state of Hampshire, the nation and world. More than 16,000 students from all fifty states and seventy-one countries engage with an award-winning faculty in top-ranked programs in business, engineering, law, health and human services, liberal arts, and the sciences across more than 200 programs of study. As one of the nation's highest-performing research universities, UNH partners with NASA, NOAA, NSF, and NIH, and receives more than $110 million in competitive external funding every year to further explore and define the frontiers of land, sea and space.

More and more Business Angels tend to join networks and build up associations. This is to ultimately diversify investment risk, by accessing high quality investment opportunities and co-investors to syndicate investments with. Angel investors part of networks and associations therefore benefit by investing smaller amounts in a larger pool of startups and leverage a community of other experienced investors who can nurture the startup's growth after the investment.

EBAN (European Business Angels Network), is the pan-European representative for the early-stage investor community gathering over 150 member organizations in more than fifty countries today. Established in 1999 by a group of pioneer angel networks in Europe with the collaboration of the European Commission and EURADA, EBAN represents a sector estimated to invest 131.64 billion Euros a year and playing a vital role in Europe's future, notably in the funding of SMEs. EBAN fuels Europe's growth through the creation of wealth and jobs.

Jacopo Losso, director of the secretariat of the European Business Angels Network, states that over the past decade there has been an increasing interest by angel investors to generate high societal and environmental impact when investing into startup business. In 2012, EBAN launched its thematic focus group called "EBAN Impact," which raises awareness, promotes best practices and enables networking among business angels seeking positive societal and environmental change with their investment activity. Business Angels invest into startups, with the intent to contribute to measurable positive social, economic, technological, and environmental impact alongside financial returns. Angels provide "smart capital" as they share experience, relations, best practices, and build paths for partnerships between their investee companies and the broader stakeholders. Fostering angel investment activity drives the growth of the entrepreneurial ecosystem, promoting innovation and creating jobs (source: EU Commission, Fostering Business Angel Activities in Support of SME Growth, 2015   https://www.eban.org/wp-content/uploads/2015/12/Guidebook-Fostering-Business-Angel-Activities-in-Support-of-SME-Growth-FINAL.pdf).   Because business angels are the first professional investors a startup entrepreneur can have access to, they play a vital role in the innovation ecosystem. Without their investment activity, many entrepreneurs would not have access to the capital, guidance, and network connections needed to launch and grow a new business. Without their investment, many of the innovations we know of today would have probably never seen the light of day.

The business volume of Business Angels in Europe has grown from 745M euros in 2018 to 8.04M euros in 2019, before recording a slight drop to 767M euros in 2020, mostly due to the COVID19 pandemic. In 2020, angel investors were involved in over 3,600 funding rounds across Europe (initial investments and follow-on rounds in start-ups). Based on the reports provided by national federations, local angel networks, and national venture capital associations, there are approximately 34,500 active business angel investors on the European continent who invest primarily through local investment networks. The United Kingdom leads angel financing, followed by Germany and countries such as France, Spain, Finland, and Denmark. EBAN estimates that for every investment measured by an angel network or association, there are about ten times more investments which are not reported or documented publicly. EBAN estimates the entire European angel investment market to be worth approximately 7.5B euros in 2020 (8.04B euros in 2019). While 9.97 percent financed SMEs and start-ups in Europe. In the US the angel investment reached $23.9B in 2019: thirty-one percent in healthcare services/medical devices and equipment, thirty-one percent of investments go to software, seven percent to fintech, six percent to retail services, five percent to energy and four percent to biotech.

The total European early-stage investment market, which includes angel investment, VC investment in seed stages, and equity crowd funding, is estimated to be worth 13.22B euros. Business angels represent the biggest share of the investment market. This is an estimated 8.04B€ of annual investment and growing as the profile of the population choses developing independent professional life rather than working for a company with which they have scarce time flexibility and a low level of sense of belonging, two critical priorities of men and women in this age and towards the future.

Conclusions

The socio-economy has transformed in only forty years. The new profiles of people that need to pay while using on one hand and need to finance their own professional projects on the other, has an unprecedented exponential growth.

Faculty at the Belk College of Business of North Carolina at Charlotte use leadership science research to train the next generation of diverse business leaders who can fill the gap that many companies face in achieving their DEIB goals. Led by faculty, George Banks and Janaki Gooty, concepts related to DEI, #MeToo and #BLM are incorporated into classrooms at all levels; the schools embrace; faculty deliver trainings, talks, and articles across audiences on topics related to DEIB.

Savings banks collapsed in the US as they could not live up to the service requirements of their clients. The sector in Spain, for example, when through the same process when savings institutions merged with commercial banks to guarantee the deposits of all its clients.

The growing need people have to govern their own time and resources has triggered the immense and expanding alternatives of loan offers is a business that completely changes the financial sector. Although the result of this behavior is different in the different cultures and areas of the world. Traditional banks have to redefine their business Amway from being a financial service provider for clients, to a business scheme that rewards its shareholders, which is what they are really doing.

In the meantime, in western countries and markets they have to downsize their costly structure and become more efficient for the services they offer to the highly diverse profile of the population. This population is Diverse in personal financial needs (loans for consumer products, for private real-estate and investments, etc.), diverse in professional behavior to finance business ideas, to set up self-employment schemes, and to set start-up ventures.

BBVA Bank in Spain closed 530 offices and downsized by 3,800 in 2021, while La Caixa fired 8,201 employees, 16.3 percent of its workforce; and Santander bank is franchising its branches in smaller cities or towns to reduce overhead and remain open to external professionals who in turn look to set up their business venture with a known brand.

U.S. banks stand to shed 200,000 jobs, or ten percent of employees over the next decade as they maneuver to increase profitability in the face of changing customer behavior, according to banking analysts. "This will be the biggest reduction in U.S. bank headcount in history," Wells Fargo analyst Mike Mayo told the Financial Times.

In 2022, Deutsche Bank was preparing to terminate 20,000 employees in Germany and United States while the bank has posted a thirty-two percent increase in profits in India.

At the same time, Shanghai Trust, Cinda, CCB, and the China Banking Regulatory Commission (CBRC) declined to comment on the fast-growing twenty trillion yuan ($3 trillion) industry, whose lending operations are cloaked behind opaque structures, and will be tough to rein in, according to employees at some trusts.

The diverse profiles of people are transforming the way of life, of work, and of financing personal and professional needs all over the world, according to the cultural behavior of the population in the different areas of the planet. There is a constant process of reinventing companies and institutions to avoid obsolescence on one hand and identifying opportunities on the other to advance with sustainable development towards future changing scenarios where cyber currencies will play unexpected dominant role.

Nestor Kreimer, a recognized financial analyst states: "Today it is already possible to live not only with the fruits of investments around crypto currencies, but by the simple fact of playing winning prizes that are monetized daily in this new cryptographic environment. The acquisition of power and independence of each individual to create value without being subject to central authorities configures a world in which each individual becomes the main actor in his or her life. From this perspective, the ownership of your heritage is no longer just economic, but all the information that due to your human condition is your own, you will now be able to control it autonomously."

El Salvador is the first country to adopt Bitcoin as a legal currency on September 7th, 2021.

The European Union Central Bank plans to launch the EU crypto currency as a stable coin by 2023.

Anthony Welch and Theresa plan for the three million square meter island of Vanuatu archipelago between Australia and Fiji to be shared by 21,000 cyber investors to become the world capital of cyber currencies.

CHAPTER 6

Future Trends:
The Future Began Yesterday

Any group of people, whether public or private in the activities they aim to achieve; will be sustainable and will fulfill its objectives only if it is able to anticipate the transformations of future scenarios. Currently, the need is more pressing, given the speed of the changes that transforms all actors in all areas of activities as well as the diversity they generate. As mentioned before, the impact of technology transforms the way of living, working, and leisure, that will generate further development due to the multiple applications that these technologies have. The speed of these innovations brings obsolescence to tools, articles, products, and services that have been used on a daily basis or brings unexpected innovation. A very current example is that of drones, which in the space of months are used every day to perform tasks that were usually done by other tools or persons, whose performance has become totally obsolete. These innovations transform the entire business and associative map, forcing the closure of companies and organizations that have not known how to integrate these technological innovations into their business model. This is the case of the press, which soon lost many of its customers, because new readers prefer the digital version instead of the print version of the book. This totally changes the structure of the companies, from the financing strategies to the information content and dissemination channels. And evidently impacts the equipment cost of substitution as well as the logistics system which must be open to new alternatives. Publishers and the press have been highly damaged by the Google search engine and must reinvent themselves or die.

The transformations of the different scenarios can be anticipated by monitoring critical indicators in the environments that set trends and identify fundamental changes. A magnificent source of information in this respect is *Tendencias21*, an independent electronic publication edited by Global Media Digital that collects the main strategic advances in science, technology, society, and culture. Since 2019, *Tendencias21* has been associated with Editorial Prensa Ibérica for the dissemination of scientific culture to the public in general. The magazine is part of what is known as "intelligent journalism," whose main mission is to offer meaningful content that allows readers to strategically position themselves in those fields of knowledge that are useful for their personal and professional positioning and development.

Tendencias21 is therefore a scheme of intelligent journalism applied to the knowledge and dissemination of science in its broadest sense, since it offers an interdisciplinary vision that integrates not only the most diverse branches of scientific research, but also the most significant advances in the schemes of thought in all types of organizations. It is also an Internet product that is subject to the basic characteristics of this technological support: interactivity, permanent updating, universality, and linkage (hyperlinks) with a series of similar initiatives that are on the World Wide Web.

Globalization benefits and affects equally companies of all sizes and areas of activity. There are 230 million companies operating in 200 countries and they have to assume that their internal market is the world. Only in Europe there are 23 million SMEs (under 250 workers), which represents 99% of the business fabric and create twenty-five million jobs. Small and medium-sized companies are a key element for social and economic sustainability of the European Union and in all other economically developed areas of the world. The bad news comes from the result of research carried out by the European Institute for Managing Diversity in 2009 for Directorate General V of Labor and Social Affairs. It showed that SMEs have only a three percent of awareness of the impact of diversity on their organizations. That is, there was practically no awareness that their workforce is diverse, regardless the number of employees in their companies. This is very critical when SMEs are the main employers in the EU, as well as in other economically developed areas of the world. This lack of competence reduces their strategic capacity to perform with efficiency which is always key to ensuring their positioning and sustainability in current and future changing markets.

The Observatory of Racism and Xenophobia of the Ministry of Labor and Social Affairs of Spain carried out an excellent study to analyze the impact of SMEs on the socio-economy of the country, their contributions and their shortcomings. The main result the research reflected was that the application of well-designed cultural diversity management (GDC) is an opportunity for SMEs, as they need tools to turn existing lack of efficiency generated by differences of their personnel into an asset to contribute to bottom line results.

The project, "Management of Diversity in the Labor Market" (GESDI) carried out in 2011 focused on working directly with professional environments such as companies, business organizations, and other agents interested in implementing diversity inclusion management processes in their organizations. Indicators on equal treatment, non-discrimination, human resources, communication, commitment, and organizational processes were agreed upon as self-diagnostic tools that open the way to the analysis of the current situation of the management of cultural diversity. On the basis of these indicators, more than thirty organizations whose cases were published in the report were evaluated. Examples of good practices which were the causes of their success and sustainability were described.

One of the results of the project was the development of a guide with practical cases, since the inclusion and management of cultural diversity represents one of the challenges that SMEs will face in the coming years. Connecting, collaborating, learning, and sharing are goals of a smart and prosperous society. The project is ongoing by the Ministry and the information is very valuable when measuring the level at which SMEs undertake inclusion policies that help immigrants and other less favored communities integrating into the country socio-economic structure.

Today, with a highly diverse internationalized market, with the tendency to relocate, among other causes, companies and other organizations need a new agenda that allows them to tackle a positive transformation, although not without risks. It is therefore imperative for SMEs to develop the capacity to assimilate these changes, changes often greater than what they are used to handle. They must develop the competence to anticipate changes, as it becomes the key that allows the introduction of new policies, materials, and technologies to avoid obsolescence and therefore lose the fundamental ability of connecting with consumer markets.

A consumer market or world population that is under profound crisis, affects social as well as economic sustainability. The global demographic curve is unsustainable. Forecasting institutions back in 2000 already announced that within twenty years later; that is in 2020, there would be more people over sixt-five than under eighteen in developed countries. Demography growth "0" in developed countries where women work and limits time for family care is partly responsible. On the other, long-life expectancy creates an unprecedented elderly population. Germán Fernández analyzed in 2017 the concept of life expectancy and recalled that in Greco-Roman times seniority started at twenty-eight years of age. Does that mean that the Greeks and Romans were old at twenty-eight years old? Obviously not. Julius Caesar was murdered at the age of sixty-five when he still had a lot ahead of him. Life expectancy in the US has gone from fifty years in 1900 to eighty years in 2011. And, in Spain, according to World Bank data, it has gone from sixty-nine years in 1960 to eighty-three in 2014. By 2004, *Mètode*, the journal of the University of Valencia specializing in the dissemination of scientific research, published that the human being as a species is programmed to live over one hundred years, and it is even considered that it could reach 120 years thanks to the information of the human genome.

This will open new business opportunities to meet the needs of a gigantic group. At the same time, it will present critical risks, for example, for the social economy pension system, because there will not be the number of new workers entering the labor market whose contributions can cover the cost of a retired population with a life expectancy of one hundred years. In addition, robotics replace workers on assembly lines. Artificial intelligence replaces persons in administrative and management functions. So again, referring to the public pension system the need for reform is more than urgent and requires the introduction of new sources of financing. On the other hand, companies should pay social security for the number of workers who replace their robots. All person systems must establish flexible systems to allow the seniors to keep on actively working beyond country retirement age. As intellectually as well as health wise most elderly persons can afford carrying out a professional life, maybe at a lower rhythm. But essentially their experience is of critical value for organizations to develop balanced policies together with the technology driven young generating entering the workforce.

Mobility is another transformational factor that must be monitored. Talent mobility is a drain on countries that lose outstanding people seeking career opportunities when their home country does not provide them. The United States attracts talent as a result of the capacity of its organization to include individuals with outstanding competences and abilities. Germany is a magnet for workers given the country shortage of hand labor. China is an interesting challenge for people who seek new opportunities in a country which evidently has a dominant position in the world today although its work culture and quality of life are very different from that of occidental countries.

Another mobility that changes the scenarios is the migration from the south to the industrialized north in search of survival, which endangers the stability of these areas. This could be avoided if investors from developed countries promote business projects in those areas, creating opportunities and jobs that can prevent migration. This is the policy that China undertakes in Africa, for example: it manufactures the products it sells in European countries in the different African countries where they reach an agreement with the local governments. This strategy allows avoiding large logistics costs and time of delivering goods to European clients. As a result, the local population benefits from a labor education which they do not have ordinarily in the country, to raise quality of life for the local population.

Now and in the future, it will be imperative to anticipate these new scenarios in order to management them successfully, and for humanity to advance with sustainable development. A very effective tool for decision makers in companies and institutions is the methodology that John Naisbitt developed in the 1960s on content analysis and published in 1982 *Megatrends*, of which he sold over eight million copies. The author proposes a very effective system that allows companies' decision-making teams to project future scenarios for their strategic decisions. The team is made up of decision makers from different areas and departments of the company, both nationally and internationally. Emerging events in the economy, technology, society, and politics are contextually analyzed and, therefore, the team is encouraged to monitor indicators that are critical to know their impact on the markets. In the same way, this prospective analysis is rethought as the foreseen events happen or not to the degree forecasted by the team, while the future strategy is corrected.

Other authors of the time such as Peter F. Drucker, were more cerebral, or Alvin Toffler who was more guarded about the promise for the future, did not invite entrepreneurs, managers, and decision makers in general to practice the capacity to forecast possible future development, a discipline, which is elemental when setting future corporate objectives.

In present volatile times of high uncertainty and extreme changes, professional forecasters are in high demand by corporations as well as by political parties and all types of social and private institutions that need to have a road map towards the future to take critical decisions to survive in the new scenarios. The International Institute of Forecasters brings together over forty Fellows in the different fields to publish monthly.

The International Journal of Forecasting, whose editor-in chief is Pierre Pinson, is the leading journal in its field. It covers anywhere from forecasting the price of energy, to marketing and financial forecasting.

Its president is George Athanasopoulos, Professor and Deputy Head at the Department of Econometrics and Business Statistics at Monash University, Australia, who received his PhD in Econometrics from Monash University in 2007. He is in constant process of establishing collaborations with organizations, associations, and academic institutions to further stimulate the field of forecasting.

The dynamism of the changes means that future scenarios are not fixed and exact. On the contrary, they are quite the opposite; they are systemic. The future scenario is a dynamic map that expresses an expected set of behaviors of different agents in the environment that allow a panoramic vision of the most significant movements that they have already started to happen. A contextual analysis of the scenario is required, that allows decision makers to calibrate the future effect of these events and behaviors in those areas that may affect the company. This early prediction of events that may happen allows them to make early and informed decisions when these new events have a positive or negative influence on the companies.

CHAPTER 7

Unequality: Managing Gaps

Ninety-five percent of demographic growth comes from undeveloped areas of the world. While the developed countries show a "0" birth rate, fifty percent of the population of the European Union in 2040 will be over fifty years old and, at that time, Spain will have the oldest population in the world. The issue no longer is that older people are living longer, but that they age in far better physical and intellectual conditions than the previous generation. Presently, senior managers and entrepreneurs that have built the economy of world enjoys, are retiring. Also relevant are university professors and scientists that have created the unprecedented level of intelligence that has triggered creative thinking. The population now retiring are the real architects of the world today. Many are not retiring to stay home and watch TV, rather to enjoy a third professional life, with the intention of leveraging their experience and getting involved in new projects which call their attention, or, which they feel committed to, or simply have longed all their lives to launch but did not have the time or the possibility of developing.

Something that the previous generations have never felt the need to do.

Experience, according to the Cambridge English Dictionary is the process of getting knowledge or skill that is obtained from doing, seeing, or feeling things, or something that happens which has an effect on you. Thus, experience is a lifetime project that cannot be trained or bought. It is an extremely valuable asset of any organization. And the retiring population is rich in experience.

Lucent Technologies, founded in 1996 as a spin-off AT&T, was absorbed by Alcatel in 1996. Back in the late nineties, it established a program designed for people over forty-three years old, because they had realized that at that age, employees began to worry about their future and about their economic and professional status once they reached retirement age. And this concern greatly reduced their productivity. The company designed an advisory program for this group. The objective was to have all the answers to what pre-retirement queries the community might have. Thus, they were advised what their financial situation would be when they retired, alternative opportunities to develop a post working life with the company, and on how to prepare for that third stage of their lives. This program proved extremely effective and gave an excellent result. It increased the productivity of employees who requested this support. In addition, a trans-generational mentoring project was established, whereby senior workers acted as volunteer mentors to younger ones. The project improved the level of information and competence of both youth and seniors.

Inequality between men and women tends to blur. The incorporation of women into all areas of professional activity, which had been roles historically reserved for men, is significant. Today the degree of development of countries can be measured by the rate of active participation of women in economic and political life. Women at work transforms the way of life and the family structure of developed countries. The same would happen if women worked in today´s underdeveloped countries, a very humanity raising and effective way to control the demographic curve which is menacing the planet sustainability.

André Schneider, former director of the World Economic Forum states: "Ensuring equal pay for men and women is crucial for all global economic agents to promote the integration of all kinds of talents and contribute to the competitiveness of companies." Emerging new ways of working may increase the birth rates in developed countries. Among the many impacts it will have in external agents is that new types of demands for products and services and well as new ways of buying will emerge. As women and men distance work, they have time to take over household tasks that now need external help, while there will be a major change in the ways of selecting and buying products for personal and family use. It is important to recall that women decide the purchase of eighty percent of products, goods, and services. This means that the tastes and needs of women condition the level of innovation and production of companies to be competitive in accelerated changing markets, which in a circular economy implies that companies that do not have women in decision-making positions risk not connecting with the real tastes and preferences of the prevailing profile of the purchasing market. Which will result in a weak competitive position for the company.

Technological talent is critical for current and future scenarios and attracting this talent at is source is very effective for the company. GenZ is the program that, since March 2021, was launched by PwC Spain to embed female intelligence in the consulting team of the organization. This strategy evidently benefits both the company and its clients.

STEM talent adds value with scientific discipline to serve organizations. Ninety-five percent of the students confirm their intention to join the firm, as it opens new opportunities for the development of their professional career. This is one more activity of their training strategy in science and technology. The project is framed in the PwC Diversity Inclusion Program coordinated by Sandra Deltell. Women can and do have a very favorable influence on organizations' financial development. Women in upper corporate positions feel more comfortable managing long term policies, than working to obtain short term results at any price. Their intuitive preference is to incur the amount of debt that can repaid by the ordinary financial rhythm of the company. A very healthy principle that Rafael Termes proposed from his chair at the I.E.S.E. Business School in Barcelona.

The Gender wage gap exceeds 201,913 million euros, equivalent to 16.8 percent of Spanish GDP in 2018. If the employment rate of women were equal to that of men, industrial output would increase, and 2.3 million jobs would be created. This is one of the main conclusions of the seventh Closing Gap report, "Opportunity cost of the gender gap in employment," prepared by PwC, which, for the first time, gives a quantitative value of the opportunity cost of labor inequality in the Spanish economy. The report denounces the barriers that women face, which wear down their professional careers. This stunning impact on the economy is the result of the degree to which women are underrepresented and undervalued in the labor market. What is even more discriminating is that there are 5.4 percent more women than men in the workforce in this country.

In terms of employability, the gap reached twelve points in 2018 with a ratio of ten employed women for every twelve men. And at the unemployment level, the difference was of 3.3 percentage points. In terms of the wage gap or inequality, women earned an average of 5,784 euros per year less than men and have an opportunity cost of 49,502 million euros, equivalent to 4.2 percent of Spanish GDP in 2017.

Another consequence is the unequal participation of women particularly in technology positions. Families tend to provide more technical education for their sons than for their daughters.

This social behavior does not help when it refers to the need to developing confidence and self-assurance in women when choosing a technical career.

The world today needs more women in technology research that prioritize social health care to heal the population as well as environmental care to heal the decaying health of the planet in order to advance toward a true sustainable development.

According to UNESCO, (between 2014 and 2016, "only 30% of female students chose higher studies within the field of science, against 70% of men in science, technology, engineering and mathematics (STEM)." Eliminating this gap is the objective of the ASTI Foundation, which was founded in 2017. The Foundation promotes awareness of the opportunities and also of the important challenges of this era of digital transformation. A new system which will rebuild the work market. Where traditional production-based jobs will disappear and new service, leisure, and technology ones will emerge. Education will then be the key to this transition.

The immediate challenge is educating the young generation to acquire the competences and skills that will be in demand in the near future. Designing active lifelong learning to train renewed talent to create and leverage knowledge and technologies as they emerge will be crucial.

CSIS 2019 shows that women preferably focus their research on sciences that contribute to the improvement of society, that is, directly to the health of people and the planet. Similarly, Red.es (a public entity attached to the Ministry of Economic Affairs and Digital Transformation through the Secretary of State for Digitalization and Artificial Intelligence) published a magnificent info graphic called "Pioneers of technology," recognizing the contribution to development they have been made by women such as Ada Lovelace (mother of computer programming), Ángela Ruiz Robles (precursor of the electronic book), Mary Kenneth Keller (early development of the BASIC programming language), or Radia Perlman (considered the mother of the Internet).

Since the 1990s, as published by Professor Emilio García García of the Complutense University of Madrid, neuroscience specialists have carried out numerous studies of the brain that show significant differences between men and women in the functional organization of the brain and of the mental activity.

The brains of men are ten percent larger and ten to twelve percent heavier than those of women. Men have a larger left hemisphere, while in the case of woman the largest hemisphere is the right. There are also differences in the volume of the temporal plane, in the nerve cells, in the nerve fibers that join the hemispheres, etc., and all this influences the unequal behavior that men and women have. The man develops with a greater degree of specialization, greater dexterity in the spatial and mathematical order, while the woman has a greater capacity for emotions, as well as for central inhibition of impulsive acts. Women have a great capacity for contextual thinking, while men have the capacity for linear thinking. That is, women can cover more issues simultaneously and identify multiple relationships between events than men do. Men have a greater capacity of risk taking, while women are more prudent when it comes to taking risks, among many other aspects that differentiate one from the other.

It is necessary to assume that men and women are unequal. They are not the same, neither physically nor psychologically. Their ways of analyzing and solving situations vary significantly. So do their priorities. What both have is equal right of treatment and opportunities in all social and economic aspects. Men and women make up humanity and the contribution of both from their multiple differences is what guarantees sustainable development in all aspects and domains.

CHAPTER 8

Discrimination:
Social Business and Legal Imperatives

Managing the inclusion of diversity implies identifying the way in which people act to achieve transformational changes in the way of respect and valuing social differences as a mandatory mechanism to improve the quality of interpersonal communication. Abolish discrimination. The objective is to build bridges of understanding in the governance of countries and regions, increase the results of companies and institutions, and improve interpersonal relations to attain professional balance and quality of life. Unfortunately, extreme unsolved discriminations coexist in the world at all levels: the genocide in Burma, massacres in Syria, the eternal disagreement between Israel and Palestine, and devastating dictatorships in African countries, among others.

For example, in 2012 the wage discrimination in the United States between the wages of senior managers and the rest of workers multiplied by 354 in the S&P 500 companies. This practice has contaminated the corporate world globally. The severity of this discrimination has led the state of Portland to punish fiscally the companies whose executive salaries exceed one hundred times those of average workers. Age discrimination is also evident: fifty percent of the unemployed persons in Spain are over forty-five years of age. And with them the corporate world loses responsibility, experience, networks of contacts, and maturity or emotional balance, values which should not trade down in society.

Child discrimination is a sad scourge that UNESCO condemns. Two out of ten students in the world suffer bullying and school violence, and the institution warns that verbal bullying is the most frequent. But there is an alarming and dangerous increase through the Internet and social networks. Every year, there are 247 million children and adolescents in the world who are subjected to one form or another of violence in the school environment. And, as published by Domingo Chiappe in 2018, every month a child under fifteen years of age and 274 under eighteen in Spain commit suicide.

On the other hand, gender violence is a discrimination that causes 87,000 deaths a year according to CEDAL data, a crime that causes one death every 2.5 hours in South America.

As representative of Spain at the UN, Nuria Chinchilla promoted a program for the Women's Anti-Discrimination Center (CAM) in 2012 that proposes that, for any corporate or government decision-making, the 3Fs must be taken into account: femininity, family, and flexibility. This in turn will include the essential 6Cs to build a more just, efficient, and humane society: male-female complementarity, care, skills, co-responsibility, commitment, and trust.

The attitude of discrimination or inclusion towards a person is taken in seconds. It triggers a process marked by stereotypes and prejudices which can lead to automatic discrimination, or to the awareness, acceptance, and inclusion of the person when cultural, behavioral, and professional information about the person emerges that there is an awareness of its potential personal and professional contribution to the group and institution. The attitude of exclusion and inclusion of decision makers conditions the relationships between governments, companies, institutions, and finally between people of all different profiles, in one way or another. In the business world, these diversities are magnified. Today, there are 230 million companies that operate in 200 countries and that understand that their internal market is the world. Therefore, the profile of the people that participate and work in a company, for example, must be able to reflect that of its external agents.

That is, the workforce profile must be able to interact and understand the needs and preferences of its clients, suppliers, and shareholders, with administrations always in search of achieving high level of efficiency in any type of institution.

When it comes to understanding the diversity of people, it must be done on the basis of their demographic and cultural profiles, which shows that both men and women have the same diversity profiles and can suffer discrimination as a consequence of multiple diversities. The main cause of discrimination is not always necessarily gender. Age, disability, skin color, religion, culture, family situation, or even personal skills or professional competencies can become a barrier when it comes to inclusion in the company or in any community. Therefore, it is important to recognize that the same person can be in a dominant position—at low risk of discrimination—or in a subordinate position—at high risk of discrimination—on the same day and because they are in different environments. A person can be in a dominant position in his or her family environment and in a subordinate position in the company where the person works under the orders of a superior.

In the case of a selection process, it is very likely that a candidate will be rejected for more than one aspect of his and her profile: more than forty years old, a certain nationality of origin, number of children, sexual orientation, religion, or simply the way the person dresses. In spite that the determining factor when including some in the organization is on the basis of its competence and skills. The most advisable selection process is undoubtedly the blind selection, to guarantee that the decision is based on the competencies and performance of the person and their potential contributions to the organizational purposes, rather than on visual traits.

In 1952, the Boston Symphony Orchestra took a decision that would make them famous: "blind auditions." Candidates had to play behind a screen to verify that gender did not influence the evaluation. In 1997, thirty-five percent of its musicians were female, after decades without a single woman in the orchestra. A research carried out in eleven orchestras found that fifty-five percent of new hires of women were a consequence of "blind" selection process.

The greater the diversity of people and objects of their interaction, the greater the speed of the innovations that they create. Taking this for granted, the differences that the constant transformations of scenario generate can be managed to the advantage of those who identify the opportunities.

A clear example of the far reach effect that major changes have in other sectors outside the one in which an innovation has been introduced, in the creation of Apple by Steve Jobs.

IBM (International Business Machines) reserved for years the fabulous IT tool for large companies, which would transform their businesses and necessarily the way they run them, as well as the need for new talents to optimize its use. This technology barrier gave the corporate world an uncontested leadership position in all areas of the business world. Steve Jobs broke this barrier by making the Apple personal computer a reality. Job gave the people what IBM had reserved only for the large corporations. The world changed as information was a tool that ordinary people all over the world would use for personal and professional tasks. An explosion of initiatives immediately changed the scenario and the way of life of a considerable sector of the world population. The personal computer was an invention created in the garage of his adoptive parents. Steve Jobs and his team personalized the use of information technology. The explosion of knowledge was exponential, forcing IBM to also launch a personal computer and thus change its business philosophy, which no longer responded to the growing needs of people to move towards the age of knowledge, new ways of working, self-employment, and a new quality of life. The launch of the Apple computer coincided with the first day the IBM CEO went to the office without a tie. A news that made the front page of *The New York Times*. This gesture marked the end of an era of selective and restricted use of technology and ended the discrimination that IBM imposed on small and medium-sized businesses and the individuals of the world population.

Another example worth mentioning is the development of the TomTom navigator that was based on a mobile application that easily marked the location of the person and his or her route to the destination address. A best seller, the TomTom business lasted the time it took the automobile industry to introduce the navigator as one more gadget in the car. TomTom became totally obsolete. However, Carlo van de Weijer decided that he was not in the business of manufacturing a commercialized a navigator device. He knew how to turn his navigation device company into a software and data company. The Dutch tech company reinvented itself from selling browsers to the end consumer to selling software that facilitates traffic management to companies and governments. He knew how to react, identify opportunities, and reinvent a sustainable company.

The variety and diversity in the application of the tasks that drones are capable of performing perfectly illustrates the opportunities that are detected when a contextual analysis of the scenarios is made. Drones replace functions of transporting goods (and soon that of people), forest surveillance, security, espionage, and as many applications as innovative persons can think. Companies are doomed to introduce them if their businesses require mobility beyond the capacity of people to do the task. However, presently there is no educational offer to prepare professionals in this field.

Companies that serve children in developed areas of the world see their target customers diminish and their needs change, while the demand for services and care for the elderly grows. Thus, successful organizations have in their DNA to take advantage of the opportunities that open up in the environment. Any decision maker cannot expect to have the same characteristics of a product or service forever in a constantly changing market. The speed of changes creates obsolescence of the products and services and thus to companies that insist on marketing them.

The cause can be changes in user taste, the age demographic curve, new legislation, the development of a new technology, changes in commercial areas at a local and global level, emerging delivery systems, the growing virtual world, climate changes, and new situations that emerge constantly. The most aggressive competition does not come from other companies in the same sector, since they all face the same threats and challenges. Sustainability lies in knowing how to detect social and technological changes in the scenario and take advantage of them, from whatever area they may come, because they end up affecting the corporate positioning.

The diversity profiles of people create new needs and realities as technology introduces unthinkable discoveries and applications. The transformations of the scenarios make continuous innovation of public and private policies imperative to avoid obsolescence and maintain their competitive condition in the markets, even if they have to change businesses to do so. To achieve sustainability in the markets, companies need to have a diverse workforce capable of anticipating changing environments, which are increasingly accelerating.

CHAPTER 9

Regional Development.
Global Sustainability

Diversity first has a major impact on the global scenario. The political conflicts that entrap humanity by the interests of the different areas of the world are a result of their macro cultural diversities which cause the global instability that identifies this era. Therefore, the inability to accept and integrate behaviors, decisions, and actions of leaders of other territories conditions the relationships between nations and regions of the world. All of this happening simultaneously in a world where a nation or region can no longer survive in isolation. It is imperative for countries to create some kind of alliance with other areas and regions of the world to be self-sustaining and benefit from the technology explosion that challenges globally discontinuity on a daily basis. Today and in the future, information shrinks the world and tests the capacity of leaders to sustain their specific power model. The innovation capacity of one area and the production capacity of others creates an unquestionable dependence and the need to understand and value each other or perish. Resources such as food and energy, among other key resources, are presently unmanageable to meet the basic needs of a world population that has overgrown its limits of suitability. Basic resources, so fundamental for the development of peoples and nations, then become a ruthless bargaining tool that forces weak areas to pay exorbitant social and economic prices. The oil empires, for example, have historically built barriers to the development of alternative and clean energies because they do not understand that these companies are not in the oil business, but are in the energy business. Individual interests have developed the growth of alternative clean energies. And have therefore endangered the health of the planet to the limits of growth. Instead of fighting them, they should have financed from the beginning hydroelectric, wind, magnetic, solar energy, and any type of non-contaminating energy that does not degrade the health of the planet. It is essential to have a planet for humanity to live.

For centuries, the world's history has been one of armed wars between tribes, races, cultures, believes and power. Only after launching the first atomic bomb and the evidence of the total destruction that it can bring to the populations and the planet, conflicts are being waged with economic, commercial, technological, and information technology weapons, creating new forms of tension in fields such as research, economy, supply, employment, migration, education, and quality of life, at global and local levels.

To help implement policies that promote the sustainability of the regions, the IEGD developed a research tool based on indicators that identify the resources which leaders must leverage in order to make their regions very attractive for people to live, work, and invest.

The 4Is model measures the intelligence of the population by the degree of talent that its inhabitants have; talent that in turn contributes to attracting investments that create wealth in the area and guarantee sustained job creation. This model measures the capacity of the population to innovation, measured by different factors such as the number of patents that are registered, the number of projects and start-ups that emerge in different sectors, etc. And, evidently, it measures the capacity of its people to include the differences in profiles of their fellow citizens and thus form an inclusive society that can enjoy a high quality of life. It also monitors the existing social organizations that give support in the areas of education, sports, leisure, and care for disadvantaged groups to promote inclusion and quality of life.

Through the implementation of the 4Is model, the strong and weak points of social inclusion orient activities implemented by public and private organizations are detected. These regional policies and projects must be designed to contribute to improving the mechanisms to become a region or a city of preference of where to live, work, and invest.

The Almería City Council applied this 4Is model in the eight provinces of Andalusia under the direction of Óscar Palomino Gual. A benchmark process was put in place. Its objective was to rank the provinces on the basis of the capacity of its institutions to attract and retain talent in the region to guarantee its sustainable growth. The research identified Granada as the most sustainable city in Andalusia, followed by Almería, with a level of agricultural exports higher than that of the entire community and with an unemployment rate of less than four percent. A strategic plan was designed to promote those areas that needed more services for the population and more favorable regulation for enterprises to carry on their business and grow. Special attention is to critical sectors such as transport, education, and support mechanisms to improve inclusion of immigrants. The qualitative and quantitative finding of the 4Is model identifies the areas in which the local public and private institutions must develop higher levels of activities to achieve in creating an inclusive region of preference for people to come and live, work, and invest.

The four 4Is indicators were also applied in Catalonia to identify the levels of sustainability of its provinces in relation to their inclusion capacity of its population and institutions.

Aware of the need to capitalize on the cultural diversity that conform to the project of the European Union, multiple networks of cities and regions have been developed to find creative solutions to the historical conflicts between the peoples of Europe and thus build together a space of respect, progress, and innovation that can guarantee the sustainability of a growing population of 500 million peoples in peace and harmony.

The Intercultural Cities is a network of 140 cities made up of municipalities, administrations, and public and private entities whose objective is to create policies and strategies specifically designed in recognition of the inclusion of diversity as a source of development for society. Under the leadership of Irena Guidikiva, the core polity of the association is to create strategies and actions that influence directly in the inclusive politicizes of cities and regions present in the Intercultural Cities Network.

The main purpose is to exchange and implement projects that contribute to promoting an equity respectful environment for its entire population.

"Making the Diversity Advantage Real" was the seminar organized by Intercultural Cities to promote the corporate world in collaboration with the IEGD on October 18 and 19, 2012 in the city of San Sebastián. Its objective was to analyze initiatives and strategies that cities could implement to promote the business world, especially SMEs. The purpose was to enhance the benefits of cultural diversity, while promoting intercultural inclusion in cities and encouraging innovation that raise the quality of life for all your residents. Forty-three leaders from twenty-three European cities participated, one from Japan and another from Belarus, who made a great contribution to the richness of the debate and to the development of the outline for a strategic planning that each city designed as a result of the event. The program included the participation of personalities from the public sector, the business world, NGOs, innovation centers, and academics. During the seminar, a scenario was built to analyze the impact of multicultural issues that institutions must address in order win over the title of preferred city to live, work, and invest.

The key issues were, among others, diversity as a "business case" both in companies and in cities and regions; the necessary diversification of suppliers; proposing to include SMEs among the corporate list of suppliers, the introduction of innovations that small businesses can contribute to, and the creation of employment. Another key factor was the way to increase the offer for outstanding education to attract families to the city or region and thus raise the level of intelligence of the residents, which would again result in their ability to attract investment.

Another continuous activity that this network promotes is the creation of startups of entrepreneurs of all types of diversity profile. It is about the continuous creation of professional activities. Intercultural Cities encourages partnerships between local administrations and regional companies to promote activities aimed at reconciling the professional and personal life of its inhabitants.

In this sense, the academic world is crucial in the work of Intercultural Cities, as it uses education from childhood to ensure an inclusive culture from family life. It also implies continuous business training in intercultural competencies and the creation of diversity chairs in universities that can transmit expertise in diversity management at higher levels, for future leaders to implement in their organizations.

Irena Guidikova, global director of the Intercultural Cities Network, describes what inspires this institution:

> For centuries, human mobility and the resulting diversity of languages, religions, lifestyles, ideas and skills have been drivers of knowledge generation, growth and productivity but also sources of friction, conflict, exclusion and violence. Is it possible to maximize the benefits of mobility and diversity, and minimize the costs? Can this be the explicit goal of public authorities and if so, at what level(s) of governance? Can public authorities design and adopt policies and narratives that help to achieve this goal? Can the policy effectiveness and impact be measured and can the insights from this assessment be used to inspire and encourage others to adopt the approach?

> In 2008 the Council of Europe – the European continent's human rights and democracy watchdog – launched an experimental programme to try and find an answer to these questions and to design, together with local authorities, a radically new approach to managing diversity. An approach, which harnessed diversity as an asset instead of avoiding it as a threat. An approach which sought to harness the diversity advantage. 2008 was the European Year of Intercultural dialogue and it provided the inspiration for the new policy model which was

dubbed "intercultural integration". The Intercultural cities programme started with only 11 ambitious, open-minded, adventurous cities across the greater Europe…it is now a network of over 140 cities globally, from Mexico City with over 20 mln inhabitants to Klaskvik in the Faroe Islands, with 5000.

Intercultural integration is about ensuring equality de facto – equal access to rights and services for all, regardless of origin, status, gender, sexual orientation, age, social or linguistic background…It is about tailoring urban institutions and services to the unique needs of users, and making them more efficient, appealing, cost-effective and equitable by co-designing them with citizens. Intercultural integration is also about cherishing diversity, giving it space and right of say in public offices, decision-making bodies, schools, hospitals, enterprises, cultural centres, libraries, housing associations…and in all spaces of work, play and politics. But most importantly of all, it is about creating and resourcing organic processes of inter-cultural mixing and interaction in all contexts of daily life, making public officials and leaders competent to manage diversity positively, and empowering ridge-builders who have the talent and skill to bridge cultures and communities.

This approach is highly unusual in the history of public policy in democracies. Until a few decades ago, community cohesion was not an aspiration or even as a possibility, neither was dealing with cultural diversity seen as a task for public authorities.

The Intercultural cities programme has developed methodologies, policy briefs, manuals, academies, learning tools of all kinds, good practice databases, a benchmark (the Intercultural cities INDEX) and a strong community of peers to help spread the "gospel" and know-how of intercultural integration. The community of intercultural cities is a strong coalition for social change, able to advocate and promote inclusion against the odds of diversity-averse governments.

Nations and cities are not equal vis-à-vis the demands of diversity management. While weakened nation-states tend to fall prey to populist leaders conjuring the cultural homogeneity of an imaginary golden age to mobilize voters' fear of change, cities embrace diversity as a motor of development. In urban centres, the laisse faire of old is increasingly replaced by urban diversity strategies in an attempt to counter the natural processes of segmentation and segregation that foster inter-group mistrust and animosity and accentuate socio-economic divides. Today, ideological and social divides run deeper than ever. More and more people lead segregated lives, only meeting and communicating with those who think like them. Pluralist, open-minded public space is shrinking.

Urban diversity and inclusion strategies are growing increasingly sophisticated and intercultural (it no longer makes much sense to speak about majority and minorities in cities like Geneva, London and Amsterdam), less reliant on massive regeneration projects and iconic landmarks designed to attract strangers, not build communities, and more on fine-grain "eco-systemic" approaches involving inhabitants as architects and masterminds of their own place-making. The humbling of urban planners has coincided with the rise of community developers skilled in creating substantive dynamics connecting people around designing shared spaces which can foster a pluralist urban (neighbourhood) identity and a sense of belonging.

Cities like Reggio Emilia in Italy and the London borough of Lewisham, when engaging in bottom-up neighbourhood regeneration of "problematic" or unsafe areas (in many cases in the aftermath of traumatic events such as urban violence or racist murders), have found that in order to ensure a democratic and inclusive process, it has been necessary to go door-to-door with interpreters, so that people of different backgrounds and levels of mastering the local language, could contribute to the consultation process and voice their concerns without having to take part in formal meetings. Making the effort (and the expense) of involving everyone in a more than formal community consultation not only sends a signal to residents that everyone matters, but also helps shape a project which resembles the local community in more than one way.

Artists-led regeneration is a way of giving the city back to the citizens but also bringing the cities to the spotlight. Loures and Nuremberg involved famous graffiti artists in creating the mural paintings based on the stories and narratives of the inhabitants in the districts of Quinto de Mocho (Loures) and Langwasser (Nuremberg) in an attempt to change the image of these diverse and rather deprived neighbourhoods and give them a new impetus using diversity as a source of inspiration. These initiatives have successfully managed to change external (feeling of insecurity, fear of migrants) and internal (lack of self-esteem, lack of ownership) prejudice around the neighbourhoods.

In Lisbon the annual Todos festival reaches a new dimension in the always renewed interplay between urban fabric, landscape and creative energy. Each year the inhabitants of the diverse Muoraria district reinvent the present and the future of their neighbourhood through the sounds, smells, histories, dreams and hopes of the inhabitants, offering an ephemeral experience of travelling the world within a square mile, but also shaping together the physical fabric of the neighbourhood, which is after each edition enriched with urban art markers of the diverse makeup of the residents. People who live and work in Mouraria "collect it" stories and memories of their neighbours, open the doors of their homes, workplaces and places of worship. Taking diversity very seriously, Todos empowers not only people of migrant background, but has special facilities to encourage the self-expression of those with disabilities too. Conceived as a crowd-sourced cultural happening of a new genre, Todos is both curated and organically grown, an art project and a social intervention, a community therapy and an exercise in participatory democracy, an urban laboratory which is inspiring other neighbourhoods and cities in Portugal.

Designing Dublin (2010-2011) is perhaps one of the most far-reaching and iconic examples of crowdsourcing the intercultural design of a city. Driven by the desire to revitalise a fledging centre which had been deserted by the middle class, the city of Dublin launched a large-scale operation of social innovation in pace-making. The Designing Dublin team (including many volunteers from the city administration) started by trying to understand this phenomenon and then finding ways to make the centre a more vibrant, appealing and welcoming place for a wider and more diverse range of residents, visitors, urban enthusiasts, etc. Over several months the team reviewed the centre and its features, diversity, challenges, and opportunities. The project covered the entire social innovation cycle – "out of the box" thinking, desire to cross boundaries, intensive conversations with citizens of all kinds of backgrounds about their vision of the city and the features which would make the centre more attractive and welcoming (such as urban sofas and green corners in unexpected places), turning the best ideas into prototypes, real-life testing, and implementing those which were found to work.

No effort was spared to reach out to those who are usually excluded (or self-excluded) from such operations. The project kick-started new urban dynamics and consolidated a culture of inclusive inter-culturalism with the city council casting itself as a learning organization tuned into the pulse of the community. One of the most striking realizations. Designing Dublin triggered was that the best way to re-invigorate the city centre was to inspire people to step out of their routine and rediscover it in a new way through urban experiences that are unexpected, enthusing, challenging and pleasurable. In order to deliver such experiences, the city had to foster interconnectivity, collaborations, opportunities for social interaction, in other words, it had to practice inter-culturality.

In the field of business and entrepreneurship, the intercultural cities experimented with the notion of "diversity connectors" – a type of business incubators specifically designed to encourage entrepreneurs of diverse backgrounds to co-create together. Many cities – Reggio Emilia, Santa Maria da Feira, Limassol and others have created diversity hubs for business in order to harness the creative potential of a diverse citizenry.

We are still far away from the moment when intercultural integration will become the dominant policy doctrine …but this will surely happen. 21st century will be intercultural.

A very effective tool is the one used by the Anti-Rumors Network (EAR) founded by Daniel de Torres. It was promoted for the first time in Barcelona in 2010 within the framework of the intercultural plan of the city and today it is the basic tool in the fight against discrimination of the Intercultural Cities Network.

The anti-rumor strategy is designed to act in diversity narratives based on prejudice and false rumors. In fake news, this can be used in populist messages that stigmatize diverse socio-cultural groups and make it difficult for them to be included in the socioeconomic system of countries and regions. Anti-rumor agents invite "read" through the false message and discover the real message which truly intends to fight prejudices and not the other way around. It is a powerful tool to encourage this change in attitude and prevent fake news from misleading people's judgment. The Anti-Rumor Manual, published by the Council of Europe and which has been translated into over a dozen languages, including Arabic and Japanese, includes the methodological approach of the strategy as well as a best practice of its system at work in different cities.

Another network is the Eurocities Network made up of large European cities that brings together 130 cities from thirty European countries. The network involves its governments as well as public and private institutions to join great movement that has become a valid interlocutor with the European Union as well as with the administrations of each country. It promotes solutions to existing economic, social, or environmental problems.

The Smart City network is promoted by ML Martínez and was founded in 2016 with twenty-five cities. By 2020, it already had sixty-five new participating city members. Its vision is "to be a global platform recognized for the quality contribution it gives to external agents." Its mission is "to connect different smart cities in a partnering ecosystem to share and create business opportunities." Its values are "to seek excellence from our creators of wealth while holding a strong commitment to the welfare of customers, partners, members and employees."

The Cities of the Future network is a roadmap for administrations to successfully advance in sustainable development towards 2030. What the future of cities will be after the COVID-19 turmoil is unpredictable, but that moment without precedent certainly opens the door to new ways of thinking and doing. Route Fifty (Government Executive Media Group digital news publication) hosted a virtual event during which an impressive number of city leaders disclosed their creative thinking to turn new ideas into actions and reality.

The fundamental emergent need to constant redesigning of the surrounding environment has led to the emergence of networks of cities and regions to manage the growing diversity of their population profile, and thus guarantee a sustainable positioning in future scenarios.

CHAPTER 10

Diversity Science.
Research Inclusion and Efficiency

Through the different empirical studies proposed in line with these objectives, the European Institute for Diversity Management, under the direction of Dr. Gonzalo Sánchez Gardey, PhD, from the University of Cádiz, set out to go in depth regarding the analysis of a series of diversity dimensions on which there is still no consensus in the scientific community. The complexity of this issue makes it especially important to start from a rigorous review of works previously carried out by different researchers and groups interested in this matter. Dr. Sánchez Gardey has always proposed this way of joining the scientific debate and contributing with evidence obtained from the Spanish reality, an area in which a limited number of scientific studies on this matter have been developed.

The analysis of the consequences of diversity in the workforce is one of the most recent fields of research in the organizational field. Its short evolution has also been marked by a vertiginous development, which has given rise to a current panorama characterized by the dispersion of approaches and conclusions. Thus, one of the basic characteristics of any research that wants to be carried out in this field must necessarily be multidisciplinary, as this is the only way to study diversity in all its complexity.

Reviewing the specialized literature, it shows that the interest in the diversity of human resources crystallizes as a line of research at the end of the eighties and the beginning of the nineties, as the social, economic, and demographic transformations found in the basis of this phenomenon is beginning to be perceived as a permanent trend. From the analysis of the first works that incorporated diversity of all citizens, as well as from their working position as human resources, the debate focusses on the organization of companies and their strategic management. Therefore, the importance as drivers of this line of research, the reports from Ahlburg and Kimmel, 1986; Johnston and Packer,

1987; Offerman and Gowing, 1990; IPD, 1996) is clear as Dr. Sánchez Gardey alludes in his thesis.

Increasing demographic diversity introduces new research questions that require a more pluralistic orientation. The depth of the change posed a very evident challenge to the previous organizational paradigms that, in the opinion of Glynn, Barry, and Dacin (2000), tended to offer homogenizing explanations, emphasizing the search for unifying principles to favor consensus, legitimacy, or identity (Eigel and Kuhnert, 1996). The first works that began to respond to this heterogeneous need came mainly from American and British publishing environments in the early 1990s.

Thus, we find some works that can be considered pioneers in this field, the first attempts to offer an explanation of the consequences of demographic diversity in organizations from researchers such as: Tsui and O'Reilly (1989); Cox (1991); Cox and Blake (1991); Tsui and Ashford (1991); Ross and Schneider (1992); Jackson and Álvarez (1992); Wiersema and Bantel (1992), or Watson, Kumar and Michaelsen (1993). From this point on, especially in the 1990s, the number of works devoted to the analysis of diversity experienced an exponential growth, tripling the number of articles and scientific works from 1970 to 2000.

The breadth of the diversity of human resources as a research problem favored the dispersion of specialized literature on the subject from practically the beginning. Despite the important advances in the delimitation of the concept or in the explanation of the effects of heterogeneity, the proposed models were developed from very different research perspectives, which has complicated the integration of propositions and the comparison of results. Reviewing the first models that were proposed throughout the nineties, it can be seen that this lack of consensus is specified, basically, around four aspects: the concept of diversity, the level of analysis of the different works, the theoretical foundations that support the different models proposed, and the objectives that guide each of the research projects.

Very different definitions of diversity can be found in literature, as mentioned above. Although the idea of heterogeneity underlies a series of demographic factors in all of them, the attributes selected in each of the cases to make up this construct are very different (Jackson, Joshi, and Erhardt, 2003). Thus, it is possible to find works that focus their analysis on the heterogeneity of the workforce in relation to aspects such as gender (Kanter, 1977; Acker, 1992; Mills and Tancred, 1992; Ibarra, 1992 and 1993; Dickens, 1998), ethnic origin

(Cox and Blake, 1991; Fujita and O'Brien, 1991; McLeod and Lobel, 1992; Cox, 1993; Watson, Kumar and Michaelsen, 1993; Ibarra, 1995; McLeod and Lobel, 1996; Ng and Tung, 1998), the age of the workers (Waldrum and Niemira, 1997; Richard and Shelor, 2002) or the presence of employees with some type of disability (Baldwin and Johnson, 1994; Cleveland, Barnes-Farrell and Ratz, 1997; Jones, 1997; Klimoski and Donahue, 1997; Dibben, James and Cunningham, 2001).

Even, at times, the heterogeneity factors considered have gone beyond demographic attributes, in the form of non-visible attributes of a psychosocial nature, such as cognitive abilities, values, proactivity, or aversion to risk (Allinson and Hayes, 2000; Brickson, 2000). Finally, in models such as those proposed by Finn and Chattopadhyay (2000), the diversity has been understood as a multidimensional reality that combines different demographic attributes whose effects are jointly analyzed. The proposed models also coincide at different levels, which shows the dispersion of the literature and research on this topic. Although the most common are developed at group level (Milliken and Martins, 1996; Harrison, Price, and Bell, 1998), diversity has also been analyzed from the point of view of the individual (Brickson, 2000) or of the organization (Richard, 2000).

The third conclusion that emerges from the analysis of the origin of the scientific treatment of diversity in terms of human resources is its marked interdisciplinary nature. As might be expected of a social research issue such as the one at hand, the theoretical foundations from which the first explanatory models were developed have also been very different. Following this pattern, to analyze each of the dimensions that this organizational reality encompasses, theories that have their origin in fields as different as sociology, organizational psychology, group behavior or strategic management have been applied (Jackson and Ruderman, 1996)).

In order to reorganize the different contributions made, authors such as Richard and Johnson (1999) or Jackson et al. (2003) have raised some revisions of the models. From all of them, it is clear the need to deepen the analysis of the academic development of the discipline and to assess the degree to which the different contributions can be integrated into an interdisciplinary model that, as suggested by Milliken and Martins (1996) or Benschop (2001), explains the effects of diversity, as well as the extent to which they can be managed.

CHAPTER 11

The Method. Corporate Global Strategy

In environments of increasing speed of transformations, it is imperative to put policies in place that contribute to the sustainability of organizations, whether they are companies of all sizes or public and private institutions. Given the need to create systems to ensure their effectiveness, companies and institutions must develop methods that respond to their structures in order to establish a corporate strategic plan that includes managing the inclusion of differences that are predominant in present and future scenarios.

The main mission of companies that make up a Diversity Council is to promote the design of diversity inclusion management models that respond to their different types of business. In the case of the Adecco International Group, which has expertise in the selection of talent for the corporate community, this modeling is even more crucial. Human resource selection must match the diverse profiles of the candidates that each Adecco client needs in order to build a truly efficient workforce.

The diversity model that guides the Adecco Group's business policy adds value both for Adecco as well as to the client companies for which the selection is made. The principles that rule Adecco diversity policy are:

- Legal compliance. Comply with national and European Union regulations and directives on equal opportunities, diversity, and labor integration.
- Talent management. The objective of the global strategy is to value corporate diversity as an element that enhances talent management in the Adecco Group (attraction, retention, and promotion of talent).
- Relationship with stakeholders. Create a diversity management model aimed at defining and improving the relationship with the main stakeholders.

- Equal opportunities (HR). Create policies and a work environment that promote equal opportunity for current, potential, and PASS employees.
- Labor integration. Create initiatives and mechanisms that favor the labor integration of people in high risk of discrimination and exclusion from the labor market.
- Positioning of the Adecco Group. Become a reference to the business community in the area of talent selection and inclusion.

Today and towards the future, an organization needs to hold a strong commitment in creating a diverse workforce as a basic strategy that guarantees sustainable growth in vulnerable environments. When a company has a diverse and highly inclusive workforce, it can take advantage of the different characteristics of the profiles of its persons and turn this multidimensional workforce into the most valuable asset of the organization. An asset, which is part of its own corporate foundation and mission. It is a tool to optimize the constant changes of the scenarios and develop proactive policies that preserve a sustainable position in VUCA environments, which are volatile, uncertain, complex, and ambiguous, as well as diverse.

According to a research carried out by the IEGD, in Spain only twenty-six percent of companies believe in the value that the personal culture of their workers adds to the business intelligence; a critical factor required in generating profits. These companies operate on the corporate principle that cultural diversity is a crucial value for the organization, which improves behavioral patterns and other levels of effectiveness. However, fifty-four percent of companies do not encourage the contribution of ideas by their employees. Twenty-six percent are totally against granting permission for the persons to think outside of the corporate behavioral patterns; or contribute with their opinions and ideas on issues that affect the traditional essence of the organization.

Three consequences result from this behavior, which directly put at risk the sustainable development of the organization in increasingly volatile environments.

- The management team is solely responsible of the promotion of business strategy innovation, which is usually more focused on generating short-term results. Too often, to maintain leadership, the management team is not inclined to analyze possible future scenarios in order to identify opportunities that can contribute to profound long-term business changes.

- The profile of the workforce must reflect unquestionably that of its external agents, especially that of clients and suppliers. Otherwise, the essence of the communication between the different steps of the process that vertebrates through the organization will fail. The cost of this human error is simply too high and has a negative impact on corporate bottom line.
- A huge loss of talent is generated. Therefore, opportunity to define more efficient and innovative processes account for added costs, both in the creation of products and services for the external clients and agents, as well as in the resulting lack of productivity of in company management systems. Once again, the power of difference entails proposing creative solutions to sustain leadership positions that can be sustainable towards the future.

The leaders of the United States Railroad Company in the late nineteenth century failed to see that they were not in the railroad business, but rather in the transportation business. They tried to stop the emerging aviation as a transport system for people and merchandise. They of course lost the battle, because evolution cannot be stopped. The US Railroad Company should have financed the development of aviation since its start, and the company would have sustained a unique leadership position in global transport and travel to this date. Organizations that insist on replicating their traditional strategies become obsolete. Organizations that try to market their products and services unchanged in evolving markets, fail.

Consumers change profiles at an unprecedented speed and therefore demand new features from products and services. This requires a constant capacity of innovation from the people of any organization to keep the competitive position of the organization in any market.

If New York Central had financed aviation, it would possibly be the world's transportation leader today. The same applies to petrol companies, since they are not really in the oil business, but in the energy business. If the powerful petrol companies would have financed alternative energies as the basis of their business since the last century, the world would not suffer the exorbitant degree of pollution that today threatens the existence of humanity.

In the radical change of scenario created by the pandemic, the hotel sector has not realized that it is not in the tourism business but in the lodging business. They should develop offers for existing housing needs in the market, such as schools and hospitals that need more space, space for job sharing activities, and: habitats for people who live alone. Esteban Ortiz-Ospina reports that "in the US, the share of adults who live alone nearly doubled over the last fifty years. This is not only happening in the US: single-person households have become increasingly common in many countries across the world, from Angola to Japan, with: 600.000 currently in Spain.

Corals Hotels in the Canary Islands has identified this trend and taken advantage of this opportunity with an excellent strategy. Currently, the seven Corals Hotels are over booked when most of the Canary Islands hotels are either closed or operating at a loss. Corals Hotels now rent suites with all professional and information technology services to clients that distance work. Professionals from all over the world who want to live in a paradise with excellent temperature all year around by the seashore take the advantage of these opportunities.

It will be very difficult for certain organizations to sustain their leadership position without constantly introducing customized innovations that keep their products and services young to connect with the changing needs and profiles of the population. The changes in behavior of the different agents in the scenarios do not leave gaps for other organizations to occupy. On the contrary, they affect and force all other agents and organizations to transform in one way or another. For example, a change in the legislation that forbids the use of red plastic material for footwear articles, not only affects footwear manufacturers; but also has a deciding impact in suppliers of materials, companies related to products and systems for pigmentation, logistics of footwear distribution, physical or virtual sales outlets, as well as distribution channels in other regions and countries for new users who have different preferences, etc. It could also force companies to disappear if they cannot reposition themselves in the markets. This change in legislation not only would then affect companies in the same footwear sector, as they are all in the same vulnerable possible. But it can affect and impact companies in all different collateral sectors. Any change can have an overall economic effect.

Discontinuity generally does not come to a footwear company from another manufacturer of the same product, but generally, from an external agent that has an equal impact in all companies in the sector.

The major competitors of GOOGLE are not Microsoft, Bing, Internet AO, Baidu, Netflix, YouTube, or Facebook. What can made it lose its dominant position is legislation in areas of the world such as China, the European Union, or the former USSR and the present Russia, who limit and regulate their activities and services.

The method proposed by the IEGD to manage emerging differences in the scenarios is a roadmap, a very effective process to introduce and sustain an active corporate culture of inclusion and diversity management as a "business case". A model which is constantly monitoring its contribution to corporate results. And a process that, in addition, improves the social environment of the organization and optimizes its technological resources as a result of the participation of all the people in the organization, regardless of size of the company or whether it is a public or private entity.

Research carried out in Spain by the IEGD in 2016 reflects the negative attitude of the institutions towards the need to include their workforce in corporate thinking. In Spain, only eighteen percent of companies establishes a knowledge generating environment to give a formal dimension to the process that generates innovation by enhancing the different areas of the organization and enrich the creation of future diverse projects. Thirty-two percent of the companies researched understand that it is an important function that should be carried out, while forty-eight percent have no record of their experiences or memory of the value that the diversity of its human resources contributes to the organization. When it comes to generating new ideas, only thirty-seven percent of companies in Spain admit and count on their people as a source of creativity when proposing and implementing new ideas. Thirty-four percent believe that the implementation of new ideas is a characteristic strongly moderated by the workforce in general, while twenty-eight percent totally dismiss the need for new initiatives as an activity that the workers are responsible for.

While in the United States, AACSB reports that, "Muma College of Business partnered with community business leaders, the Tampa Bay Lightning and Jabil, to create a certificate program to educate business and community leaders on essential practices and tools for increasing employee diversity and creating a business model that embraces equity and inclusion." This is a movement to guarantee that these future corporate leaders will implement DEIB (diversity, equity, inclusion and belonging) policies in the organization they will create or work in their professional lives.

It is not surprising, that only nine percent of companies have established strategies that encourage people to formulate suggestions that can then be turned into projects that contribute to the success of the organization. This attitude on the part of the management of twenty eight percent of companies reflects a dramatic resistance to change and a corporate culture that creates barriers and does not "give permission" to the launching of new proposals by the workforce. This is a mistake; since creativity is a consequence of the permission decision making give all members of the organization to formulate new proposals as a result of their differences of culture, education, and experience. These differences are at the root of the capacity of individuals to contribute and be an active part of a sustainable market position for the company in current and future very dynamic scenarios.

CHAPTER 12

Corporate Commitment: Economic and Social Mission

Managing the inclusion of diversity in an organization is a commitment of all the members in upper management positions, their behavior and decision-making. Managing the differences of human resources cannot be restricted only to certain areas of the organization and not to the rest of the company. The business process requires ethical behavior, professional skills, efficient communication strategy, high level of equity behavior, as well as fair and effective compensation policies. Incentive programs cannot be created just for a specific profile of workers, because the company would then be responsible for positive discrimination, which will create conflicts and legal demands.

#TalentoSinEtiquetas is ADECCO Diversity and inclusion corporate strategy that declares that all persons have equal rights and that every person is unique. The organization clearly anticipates the future of the employment sector and creates an innovative model that relates to its relations with clients, to its candidates, and to society in general. These are the principles that rule the company and set the vision of the style of its business performance, its way of acting, of understanding, and of leading the labor market. This initiative is embedded in the Adecco Diversity Committee of Spain, led by Encarna Maroño and Francisco Mesonero, and represented in all the corporate business lines (service, commercial, human resources, communication, corporate responsibility) with the objective of establishing diversity as a fundamental value of the company.

In the same way the project is a reference for all Adecco international companies "We disregard all standard ways, in order to create a new human resource selection model centered a hundred percent on the talent of the candidates in order to guarantee a service that adds value to the labor force of our clients. Always complying the legislation, with relation with groups of interest, guaranteeing equal opportunities with the maximum labor integration that can assure the leadership positions of the company in global markets regarding all aspects of diversity and inclusion management and talent selection."

Rosa Alarcón Montañés, president of Trasportes Metropolitanos de Barcelona (TMB) established in the 2020 Corporate Report, "Thanks to the implication of all persons, we have accomplished an excellent level for all that is fundamental to TMB. The constant efforts to respond to the needs of our citizens, has not distract us from other very important objectives such as the respect for the environment and the need to improve quality of the air. We work in an inclusive way and with the aim of developing constant innovation and constantly improve the transport services we give the local population. A commitment that now more than ever makes TMB an essential part of Barcelona and its metropolitan areas."

Scenario Building for Future Strategic Planning

For corporations to be sustainable in present and future environments, mid-term and long terms focus must be very clearly established and shared by the management team. The opportunities must be detected as well as how to equip the organization to achieve a leadership position as it advances toward future changing scenarios. Because the future began yesterday, limiting action to managing present markets brings obsolescence to the company. Therefore, the management team must systematically analyze trends and construct foreseeable scenarios that alert the organization in order to identify new diverse profiles of clients and suppliers, of changing legislations and economic behaviors. Then the decision makers must constantly design strategies that will make the organization sustainable as the scenarios change.

Amancio Ortega and his wife Rosalia Mera started hand sewing quilted robes which later sold door to door until in 1972 their brother-in-law, Jose Antonio Caramelo helped them to finance the first ZARA store and set up what today in Inditex is one of the largest companies in the world with 6,477 fashion retail stores. Inditex has made an important shift towards the real estate business to sustain corporate profit margins. This does not mean that it gives up having a leadership position based in the principle of delivering quality design fashion tailored to the profile of customers of stores in different parts of the world. The fashion offered in a New York Fifth Avenue store is not the same as the one offered in a retail store in Vigo. ZARA will keep on innovating and delivering tailor made fashion to consumers all over the world because a very well-articulated system allows them to deliver lasting fashion in fifteen days to all their diverse clients. Detecting fashion trends, managing suppliers and production systems, capitalizing on very create logistics to deliver in record time, and sustain the highly efficient system on which the corporation basis its very singular offer contributes to their success.

Moreover, owning the real estate of the stores can better regulate the profit margins, compensate the currency vulnerabilities, the variation in the demand as well as the strategies for global production.

The economic chaos created by the pandemic can highly affect the company´s financial sustainability. Inditex will have to rethink its real estate empire in order to redefine its largest source of income in an uncertain future scenario where physical sales in stores and the potential virtual market as preferred fashion purchasing channels will be redefined.

Anticipating future scenarios is an art, which companies need to master if you want to anticipate and prepare for major changes that will foster alliances between regions all over the world which in turn will open very different environments in which to develop. All the companies which operate in the same sector face the same challenges. Therefore, analyzing the movements and trends of future scenarios implies obtaining a broad vision in the direction towards where the company may potentially advance so that the mega-changes operate in their favor rather than against company interests. So that the inclusion of the diverse profiles of the employees today will guarantee the development of abilities and competencies which will contribute to sustain positions of leadership as scenarios transform toward the future. Upper management must bet for those activities, which can provide a higher operating margin, excellent and diverse talents to implement new policies.

In the sixties, the glass containers gave Gervais an ample competitive position. The company later decided to buy the glass container supplies as the container represented the highest cost of the product. The company kept implementing this policy as other types of containers were used to guarantee the quality and innovation of the product. Buying the suppliers of the new type of containers Gervais uses for the products is another alternative policy to controlling the costs and margins of the products always offering the highest quality.

Ray Kroc, founder of McDonald's, claims that the corporate benefit of the franchisee of fast-food establishments is not on the sale for burgers, but in the rental of the location to the franchisors. The McDonald's empire has extended to all continents. The burger offered is adapted to the culture and tastes in every country. The burger offered in Moscow does not taste the same as that offered in Beijing, Spain, or Bombay. What really sells is its brand, its corporate policy, and its business structure based on select localization.

Diversity Council

A diversity inclusion policy is a corporate strategy that affects the entire structure of the organization. It is the responsibility of a person or team that responds directly to the maximum management level of the organization and its efficiency must be measurable both by tangible and intangible parameters.

Who leads the team, the committee of the Diversity Council should form a group of people who represent all the areas of the organization so that its members develop and transmit a sense of belong to the organization. This structure automatically establishes interactive communications with the entire workforce of the company. To disseminate information, announce projects and opportunities that equally reach all members of the workforce, and establish feedback channels to receive responses, suggestions, and queries from all the employees of the company.

Sandra Deltell Díaz, PwC Spain Social Inclusion and Diversity Officer, declares that the corporation holds D&I is a key objective for business development: "Since last year the company has established a Diversity and Inclusion Global Council made up by senior corporate leaders who represent the different business areas of the company and ways to operate. This Council proves our firm intention of all the countries to advance in this subject in a coordinated way, and to do so starting from the highest levels of the organization. This Council is responsible setting the programs, initiatives, and policies that must be developed worldwide on one hand, and to give support to the persons responsible for Diversity in each country and in each geographical area of the world on the other, to guarantee that innovation is fostered and implemented at all levels of the organization. Back in 2004, PwC recognized diversity as a business imperative by the company international strategy facilitator. In 2015, the leadership structure and governing global bodies of the PwC network of companies have assumed Diversity and inclusion as a priority.

It is important to highlight the fact that any person in the organization is legitimated to present an initiative to the Council from its area or its branch of the corporation. Generally, when an idea or initiative is accepted, it is executed even if the person that promotes the idea does not necessarily have to belong permanently to the Council team.

A good example of personal initiatives put to practice is the Henkel and DHL corporate social responsibility project promoted in alliance with the Diverse Artists Association. A contest is organized for artists with disabilities to send in their paintings. The company employees vote to select the prizes winners, and therefore are involved in the project of which they hold ownership of. The paintings which are selected as contest winners will decorate the company's office spaces.

Henkel makes the award ceremony coincide with the corporate Diversity Week at international level.

The Barcelona Metropolitan Transport system (TMB Metropolitan Transportation of Barcelona) calls for Innovative ideas from its workforce. The core condition to participate in the program is that the idea proposed focuses on equipment and product of services that TMB could incorporate in its structure to improve the quality of the transport system as a whole. If an employee has an innovative idea, he/she will present it to the Diversity Department, and if accepted, the project promoter is allowed to recruit technicians from the different areas of TMB with the professional skills and competence needed to development the project. The teams are extraordinarily diverse in demographics as well as in cultural diversity profiles. Time and space is also allowed for the team to develop a business plan in order to present it at a corporate event together with all the other projects, TMB Innova. All the projects awarded are incorporated into the structure of the company, whether they are brakes of the trains, accessories for the bathrooms, or automatic steps to facilitate the access of persons with reduced mobility to the wagon. Manuel Barriga was the human resource manager at the time when the project was designed and launched. One year, seventy-two teams of employees presented their innovation ideas. Three of them were patented because they were new to the world. The mobility of team members from their usual working place and area, to work with other colleagues from other sectors of the company in order to put together an innovative idea of their own, is of enormous value for the development of inclusive behavior and the sense of belonging to the company. Another added value is that these employees become diversity champions and promote a sense of empathy and inclusion throughout the entire business structure.

Another very good example is that of the Bimbo Group. For the company, "The inclusion of diversity is the ability or capacity of an organization to promote the active participation of all its members in the creation of value."

It is also interesting to see how UEFA, in cooperation with FARE (Football Against Racism in Europe), promotes the campaign against racism in football, the objective of which is to transmit the positive aspects of cultural diversity, to successfully compete with the participation of major patrons of the tournament. Spain, with a very diverse team, won the Eurocopa in 2012.

Set Objectives and Indicators

Setting the objectives to be achieved is essential in order to be able to identify the profiles that the members of the workforce as well as collaborators must have, because they will be responsible of the future success of the organization. These objectives should be clearly set as they will be the indicators that will define the way of measuring the results of each project designed to foster inclusion. Company resources will therefore be correctly assigned to projects that make a higher contribution to corporate results. If a company objective is to expand to three new countries, the selection process for new workers and collaborators must established the principle of identifying candidates primarily with the competence required for the job. And then select candidates on the bases of the demographic and cultural profiles that match these new markets, in order to contribute to the future internationalization corporate strategy.

The research conducted by Paul Gompers, a professor at Harvard Business School, and Sophie Wang, proves that the probability of success of a new business that goes public in the stock market, or that is sold for a price higher than the amount invested, is three percent higher if there are women in the management team of the new company.

Otherwise, it shows that the return on inversion is only three percent superior in the case of an homogeneous team (men of the same age, same professional skills, and same level of university studies). Another finding is that the female profile has more influence that age, culture, and others different features when it comes to achieving efficiency in corporate profits.

Having a diverse workforce allows the company to assign projects to employees whose profiles better reflect customers' needs or the target population. Cluster, the Catalan mobile technology management consulting firm, in the nineties selected and recruited its people based on the profiles that could better interact with the native population of the countries in which the company had contracts and operations. Employees were included in the project management

´team with different responsibilities and functions, according to their cultural and skills contribution to the project, to ensure that the business plan not only was technically perfect but that it also respected the culture and mind set of the people of the client company in the different countries where projects were in place. Cluster was a company with an extremely high level of efficiency. A leader in its sector. In 2000, Diamond, a US corporation bought Cluster for 1.100M dollars.

Many organizations are trapped between diversity as a generator of innovation and homogeneity that condemns organization to obsolescence. It is surprising that Spain occupies the forty-nine percent place in terms of business efficiency in the world ranking, as a result of the traditional resistance to change of decision-makers in the corporate world. although there is an increasing number of entrepreneurs who are creating world leading organizations such as AIA (Aplicaciones en Informatica Avanzada). Regina Llopis, founder and CEO states,

"We constantly research, which allows us to pioneer the implementation of new solutions for all types of industries. We apply I+D so that client companies can make a difference."

A EIMD research reports that only thirteen percent of Spanish companies consider the diversity of the labor force to be a positive factor in the company. Fifty-three percent are aware of these differences but make a passive use of it, as they are considered "potentially valuable." Thirty-two percent of the companies believe that differences between people, even if they respond to the company stereotype, represent a negative aspect for the institution. Fortunately, fifteen percent of companies look for different active profiles that can integrate a work force that is not homogeneous, although sixty-eight percent can block and discriminate against ten different profiles. This behavior can be the cause of loss of business opportunity on one hand and generate conflicts on the other.

Given the change in paradigm of people that do not respond to the stereotype of the organization, that traditionally have a preference for an homogeneous workforce and hold a high resistance to change, this can drive an organization to obsolescence and failure.

Accenture is a great example of corporate commitment with diversity. Accenture, a Fortune Global 500 company, is a multinational professional services company and operates in Spain. Accenture attracting customers from over 120 countries with 469,000 employees, with a business volume of 43.2 million dollars and 1.691 million dollars profits in 2019. Julie Sweet, Accenture Advisor, and Patrick Rowe, Director and Deputy Adjuster General, state that: "In the current scenario, we will have more of a legal and professional compliment. We will innovate with the integrity of our technology and its impact on people to develop inclusive, responsible and sustainable solutions to business and social challenges. To do so, we need to connect with all our people to take the best decision, act with responsibility and communicate with assertiveness."

CHAPTER 13

Awareness: Belonging

A lifelong activity of a diversity leader is the implementation of awareness programs to foster the sense of belonging of all the members of the workforce to a common project, the socio-economic contribution the company makes to all external agents. A shared objective to which each employee must know and value his or her task that makes the entire system possible.

Messages that invite all members of the workforce to have an inclusive behavior towards all peoples of the organization, regardless their diverse profiles are necessary.

The objective is to make everyone in the institution aware of the fact that all coworkers have different demographic profiles as well as culturally different ways of thinking and performing, and that these differences can be a source of wellness for the organization as well as for each person in the company. It is therefore mandatory to emphasize that all persons have the right to have different features that make them unique. It is therefore a winning strategy to reward a behavior of social and professional correctness. Then the role of the diversity leader, or the team involved, consists in developing awareness and support programs to train all workers to appreciate and value the differences of every person that works in the company. Promoting the practice of active listening to stimulate new ideas and suggestions from all members of the personnel and train in the art of including instead of discriminating people because of their diverse physical or cultural differences becomes essential, he or she should be trained to respect and include the differences of other people in the working environment.

"The Python Software Foundation (PSF) and the Python World Community will welcome and encourage the participation of all. Our community is based on mutual respect, tolerance and self-esteem, and we are working to help the people to practice this principle. We want our community to be more diverse:

Whoever you are and whatever your training is we welcome you" says D. A. Abrams in his book Diversity and Inclusion.

Communications

When addressing communication strategies, all channels must be considered to reach everyone who is related with the organization. Combining presence, printed, and virtual activities to constantly transmit messages that encourage collective participation and the sense of belonging. Complying with the current legislation, which penalizes exclusion and discrimination must be the culture of the company. Therefore, all members of the organization must practice an inclusive behavior.

Awareness-raising training to combat partisanship or unconscious bias behavior must be a constant activity encouraged by the diversity team. Intercultural seminars, whether presence or virtual are interesting and highly effective ways.

Unconscious, also known as implicit bias training, has risen in popularity since the creation of the Implicit Association Test (IAT) that was created in 1995 by Anthony Greenwald to detect the hidden contents of the mind. The IAT is designed to be a quantitative measure of the types of biases that an individual may possess. While it attempts to give an objective measure, what it does not do is to help individuals understand from where their biases come, and what to do to reduce the negative impacts of bias.

Neuroscience is used in part to explain the biological determination of bias, and why human beings make snap, instinctive unreasonable judgments. What the IAT and neuroscience do not address is the social learning that results in the creation of certain associations. The unconscious bias training reported here, whilst it addresses the biological determinism of bias, concentrates heavily on social learning, and how certain biases are learnt and programmed individually over time through social interaction and reinforcement.

Jude Smith Rachel explains: "We believe there is tremendous value in unconscious bias training if is delivered professionally as part of a comprehensive strategic plan; tracked with solid metrics and supported by robust and consistent leadership that is also engaged in the learning process. If we are going to improve outcomes, then we suggest suppliers and companies could benefit tremendously by having several assurances in place."

1. Accreditation/validation of suppliers delivering the training and not try-ing to generically state whether courses per se are effective, unless stud-ies control for who delivered them.
2. Suppliers (or independent audits) being equipped with sufficient analyt-ical competence in building robust measurement frameworks to deter-mine workshop efficacy; and
3. A strategic long-term, sustainable commitment and approach to improv-ing workplace culture, not simply by bringing to the surface potential biases held by individual employees, but also by addressing deeper sys-temic and institutional cultural bias.

A more professional and strategic approach to unconscious bias training yields the results that companies need, and can demonstrate for them just how and where they can see a return on their investment. The longitudinal study present-ed in this chapter shows the positive impact that the training has had over time for a cohort of employees, and the enthusiasm they have for the training, and the learning that they experienced as a result. The training generated awareness, changes in behavior and a significant amount of motivation on the part of the employees to improve their relationships with both their colleagues and their clients. The unconscious bias training case study presented here shows that the training generated a significant amount of goodwill, that sadly in the absence of sufficient organizational strategy and leadership accountability, was not fully capitalized to have a long-term positive effect on the organizational culture.

CHAPTER 14

Communication: Stakeholders' Alliances

Internal communication is a fundamental activity that needs to be designed, structured, implemented, and measured throughout the organization. It is imperative to have an open communication channel to reach all the members of the organization. The mission of communications is to discuss issues and events of general interest as well as of personal development opportunities that the company may offer such as: training, mobility to other areas of the company, promotion opportunities, sabbatical time, and flexible time working conditions, exchange initiatives, voluntary social oriented projects, and other corporate initiatives.

A two-way communication and information exchange media should be set by the diversity team to channel complaints of any type of discrimination any employee may be a victim of. These incidents must be immediately addressed and shared in the area where it occurs with the other members of the department where it occurs in order to immediately undertake positive conflict solutions. A corporate learning process, which firmly embeds an inclusive attitude from all employees is necessary. The message the company must clearly transmit is that: "The people of this company do not allow discrimination,"

A researched directed by Gonzalo Sanchez Gardey, Vice Dean of the University of Cadiz disclosed that eighty-nine percent of companies do not have established information channels that allow them to increase efficiency in the organization. Only in fourteen percent of the companies interpersonal exchange is a standard practice which is the behavior that contributes to the diagnosis and resolution of problems, thirty-three percent are moderately satisfied with the work in conjunction with its workers, while for twenty-three percent this interrelationship is somewhat unacceptable- and while twenty-seven percent of the organizations admit that their employees do not contribute to improving the diagnosis and resolution of problems due to a lack of interrelationship.

It is therefore significant that in eighty-nine percent of the companies, the initiative the staff suggests increasing the effectiveness of the organization is not taken into consideration. This results in a high cost for the organization regarding innovation and inclusion of its workforce.

These plans and initiatives aim at increasing the sense of belonging of the people in the organization. A transparent communication policy transmits corporate ethical values, which add when aiming at creating a sense of partnership with all members of the organization. Consequently, the people with high levels of talent will contribute to corporate objectives with high-level performance in their respective roles, as this is the preferred surroundings for this profile of professionals. Therefore, projects of common interest will be a powerful tool in bring together the entire organization.

According to this research, in spite of the fact that eighteen percent of companies establish protocols for the transference of knowledge. Only eleven percent of the companies have established an information system that directs and transmits information between groups and areas. Consequently, this results in the loss of knowledge that affects forty-three percent of business. Only nineteen percent incorporate structures and information processes to leverage the information generated by the organization to manage sustainable leadership in highly diverse and changing scenarios.

On the other hand, fifty-eight percent value the incorporation of knowledge into processes while sixteen percent consider that it is not necessary. The workforce of seventy-four percent of the companies does not fully know the scope and range of business the company they work for. This explains that employees frequently fail to contribute to the development of the company, as well as the lack of sense of belonging many employees have toward the organization.

External communication must project principles and criteria that emulate internal communication policy. The message must clearly project the corporate culture to be shared with customers, suppliers, and external agents in general. When products or services have similar characteristics, the customers "buy" the brand, when the brand clearly expressed corporate policies and commitments. For example, in 2018, Adidas signed twelve-year sponsoring contract with Real Madrid Football Club for 1.6M euros, a club which has followers all over the world. This alliance identifies the Adidas brand with the global notoriety of the Real Madrid brand. This is an immense value for the company sponsoring the club. It is a clear business case.

A company that leverages respect and value for the differences of its people becomes a preferred company to work for and attracts young talent as well as employee that feel undervalued where they presently work.

The Communication Plan must be comprehensive and encompass all the areas and activities of the organization. Not only because it must transmit all the characteristics and conditions of its diversity inclusion project, but also because it must involve all its objective target groups in order to influence the behavioral transformation required and reach the forecasted corporate objectives.

Reaching out to the external public and stakeholders in general must be a priority corporate business objective. The communication broad spectrum includes brand alignment of all its publics. Attracting the best talent is essential for corporate development. Attracting new customers and consolidating alliance with suppliers and shareholders are other critical purpose to peruse. The company, regardless its size, must prove and convince all agents that it is inclusive, does not discriminate, complies with the antidiscrimination labor legislation and that it somehow contributes to the social and economic sustainability of the country.

CHAPTER 15

Diverse Workforce:
Mirror External Publics Profiles

Larry Summers, Harvard professor and secretary of the United States Treasury Department, coordinated significant research:

"It is a test that aims at identifying other sources of results and it ends up demonstrating that diversity is good." The priority of any organization should be that of analyzing, in all its dimensions, the profiles of each component of the labor force, and thus evaluate whether the profile of the workforce reflects that of its external social agents. When projecting the future development of the organization, it is mandatory for the workforce profile to be able to effectively interact with current as well as with future agents and potential clients for the company to be sustainable is rapidly changing environments.

Moreover, the business culture of the company should encourage its people to express new ideas and suggestion on issues that relate to the organization basic norm and that can be considered positive innovative contribution to improve the corporate process and its market positioning. The programs put in place must then be measured, so that management can evaluate the contribution it makes to achieve its objective: in this case is generating innovative ideas.

The company will be then sustainable towards the future, as the entire organization is actively innovating to keep the institution a step ahead in the market.

In the research carried out by Doctor Gonzalez Gardey, in Spain, forty-eight percent of companies say that the information flow is projected to stimulate the learning process and, therefore, determines the creative capacity of the team. Seventeen percent of companies formally establish policies that strengthen the relationship among employees, which are therefore accountable for corporate effectiveness. And fourteen percent state that team members put forward the diagnosis and styles aimed at business development and efficiency.

In the European Union, there is an estimate of twenty-three million small and middle size companies (with less than 250 workers), that create ninety-nine percent of the labor market (75 million jobs). Yet only three percent of these entrepreneurs are aware of the cultural diversity (GDC) as a management tool, a very critical finding given that the majority of the working population in the EU is employed by SMEs.

The Spanish Observatory for Racism and Xenophobia of the Ministry of Labor and Social Affairs of Spain, under the direction of Nicolás Marugán Zalba, carried out a project in 2011 under the title of "Diversity Observatory in the World Laboratory" (GESDI).

The focus of the Observatory was to research systems that enabled working directly in professional environments, such as entrepreneurial associations and other agents interested in introducing diversity and inclusion processes in their organizations. Indicators were identified to determine the level of equal opportunities, antidiscrimination, human resource management, communication, corporate commitment, and other critical issues. A self-diagnosis tools was designed to analyzes the resulting company diversity culture. Indicators were selected and over thirty companies were evaluated regarding level of diversity and inclusion policies and activities put in place. Their best practices where published. A guide of successful case studies was created. The growing diverse profiles of workers, clients, and suppliers is a major challenge that SMEs have to face in the coming years. Connect, collaborate, learn and share are objectives that an informed society must develop in order to successfully participate in global markets.

The Ministry of Labor and Social Economy in Spain constantly monitors discrimination and inequality behaviors, which stimulates promotion of an inclusive environment. The Training Manual on Diversity Management, addressed to companies of the European Union member states and Turkey was published. Diversity is the very nature of the Union. It is therefore mandatory for the different social agents of its 446 million population of highly diverse cultural profiles and demographic differences to manage inclusion.

Karoline Fernandez de la Hoz, director of the Spanish Observatory of Racism and Xenophobia, prioritizes the need to turn the menace of conflicts derived from diversity discriminating behaviors, into distinct values for the development of the business community in the European space. The Ministry specifically promotes inclusion towards the Islam community in Spain, which represents four percent of the total Spanish population and has a significant weight in the country economy. The ministry also monitors the existing Hispanophobia in different areas such as education, employment, and communication in order to promote its inclusion in the social environment. Research destined to analyze the different ways of working with communities in risk of discrimination are also conducted on regular basis by the Ministry.

To lead is to do something first. Therefore, the company needs a talented workforce with the capability of challenging existing procedures on one hand, and at the same time exceeds the offer of competitors.

Kellogg's founded a university open to all types of students from around the world who chose to be trained in the highest quality level of business education. Utmost quality and advanced knowledge training to match the corporate business needs to make a company sustainable towards the future. This is particularly important as in the case of Kellogg´s a company that bases its business in a single product. The capacity of innovation that this one hundred years old company has been extraordinary. The Kellogg`s cereal has managed to keep a leadership position worldwide during a century. Very excellent performance. Kellogg´s University is therefore the best source of human resources for the organization.

Sources

When searching for new talent, people with different and advanced professional capacities, preferably with a record of success in different sectors, who master technological advances, need to be detected from different sources. If the candidates always come from the same universities, from the same selection organizations, from the same origin, the company will always have a homogeneous workforce, which tends to obsolescence.

Professor Joseph Di Stefano of the University of Lausanne, reports that homogeneous groups tend to obsolescence, as its people tend to operate in the comfort zone and repeat strategies that have worked for them before, rather than venturing in new directions and ideas.

In this case, the company will probably fail to create the necessary level of innovative solutions to keep products and services relevant in changing and vulnerable markets. Where the search for new candidates is concerned, it must be carried out directly where the required profile of persons can be found; for example, in universities and search consulting companies of the countries where the company plans to have operations in the future.

BSN searches through different professional associations and universities directly in the countries where the company is or will be doing business in order to explore innovative profiles in other fields that may enrich the company and bring new types of competitive advantages. Always keeping an open search through recommendations made by company employees who are already familiar with the culture and leadership style of the company they belong to. LinkedIn is the biggest network of professionals that brings together the greatest number talented people of the world. With 575 million users, 250 of them actively using the network, fifty-seven percent are men, thirty-eight percent are millennial, and forty-four percent have an average income of 75,000 annual dollars, higher than the rent of the population in the United States. LinkedIn is a preferred site for detecting human resources, as well as for the development of global-level alliances.

Selection

The unquestionable principle is that employees need to have the intelligence, skills, and abilities that the company needs so that the tasks required by the business are performed with high quality levels. And they must also have diverse profiles that may contribute to achieving corporate efficiency in the different fields of the organization where they perform their task. Different demographic profiles such as (ethnicity, language, religion, sexual orientation, disability, and nationality of origin) as well as cultural profiles such as (language, belief, education, family structure, competence, and abilities) allow them to establish coherent intercultural relations with their present and futures clients as well as suppliers, and add value to the business process. Evidently, the selection process cannot discriminate based on gender, ethnicity, and belief of any candidate. The selection has to be made on the grounds of the profiles the organization needs to maximize interaction with clients, suppliers, and other key external agents for the company.

Blind selection is highly recommended although not practiced by all companies because of traditional resistance to change when it comes to incorporating persons who are different from the corporate norm.

An excellent example is that of the philharmonic orchestras.

Blind auditions, as they became known, proved transformative. The percentage of women in orchestras, which hovered under six percent in 1970 now has radically changed. Women make up a third of the Boston Symphony Orchestra, and they are half of the New York Philharmonic. Blind auditions changed the face of American orchestras.

Another example is Zety, the online curriculum editor that supports the blind CV, also known as "anonymous CV". A model created with the purpose of combating discrimination in recruiting processes. The model limits information about gender, ethnicity, nationality of origin, photos and any information that could represent a source of discrimination.

In 2017, the Ministry of Health, Consumption, and Social Welfare of Spain also implemented the use of the current or anonymous curriculum as a means of reducing discrimination, at least in the first filters of the selection processes.

The Adecco Foundation defines inclusion as "an imperative element that refers to the capacity to manage and integrate individual differences in a work team, promoting the diversity of talents, experiences and identities."

In 2018, Adecco published a report regarding RSC policy and social corporate responsibility. It announced the following information which projects a very significant behavior of the business world in Spain when contrasting with the situation in other countries: "Twenty percent of the companies have started to actively address the issue of diversity and inclusion; thirty-three percent develop some type of initiative to promote diversity and only ten percent work with blind CVs."

The European Commission calls "multiple diversity profile" a set of profiles that people have in common and that run the risk of suffering discrimination because they do not respond to the stereotype of the dominant profile of the workforce and their environment. As mentioned earlier, a person can have more than one profile that can risk being discriminated against in the selection process.

For example, a forty-five years old female candidate who has deaf problems may represent a risk when integrating into the company work process. She runs the risk of being discriminated against for the disability rather than on behalf of her gender or age.

It is very common to see that companies prioritize discrimination on the basis of disability, disregarding the professional competence of the candidates and their potential contribution to company results. It is likely that the company faces the cost of loss of creative talent and business opportunity by discriminating against candidates with the correct professional competence but with diverse cultural and demographic profiles to those of the company standards.

The goal in any selection process is to attract candidates that combine professional high standards with personal features that can contribute to the present and future development policies of the organization.

Russell Reynolds is an international company with high expertise in quality talent selection. Its strength lies in the capacity to understand the corporate policy of the clients and match the profiles of the candidates to the requirements of the company during the selection process. Russell Reynolds then puts together a menu with the profiles of the preselected candidates so that the corporation can choose the one that can make a higher contribution to the objectives of organization.

Over 600 million passengers a year depend on Barcelona Metropolitan Transport system as a means of mobility. Raquel Díaz, Director of Diversity, explains that TMB has the commitment of selecting and creating a workforce that mirrors the social reality of the community of people that use any of the different types of transports that the company offers, and takes good care to meeting the clients' cultural differences, behavioral style, origins, features, etc. The selection is based on preferred professional competence for the specific task and in the second place the value added by the diverse characteristics of the candidate to meet the needs of the highly diverse daily users of the transport system in Barcelona.

> The company bases its process on its capacity to integrate people with diverse profiles, because the TMB workforce is highly diverse. COVID-19 validated this corporate policy and principals. Only organizations that are ruled by this principle are capable of detecting opportunities where great risks also menace. TMB is in a constant search for persons capable of reinventing business activity, surviving and succeeding in highly convulsive and unpredictable scenarios.

Diversity Profiles

The academic world classifies the diversity profiles as demographic and cultural, as mentioned before. An iceberg is a very clear way of illustrating the types of profiles as well as the difficulty to analyze their impact in interpersonal relations. In the iceberg, the visible or demographic profiles are above the waterline and the invisible cultural profiles are under the waterline. A simple interpretation of the graphic is enough to appreciate that dealing with the different profiles requires different inclusive behavior. Demographic profiles can lead to a spontaneous appreciation of a person, on the basis of gender, ethnicity, disability, sexual orientation or appearance, and have an immediate reaction on the observer that responds to the stereotype of what is correct or incorrect, what is right and what is wrong, an attitude that is acquired in childhood. This accounts for the fact that a person can include or discriminate a newcomer in the first seconds of meeting, because the person is reacting instinctively responding to almost innate perceptions toward other persons. Unconscious bias is very frequent, and generally the person is not aware of this behavior. Cultural profiles are those that require knowing the person, which involves talking to them, exchanging opinions, and research information related to the way of life of the person. Cultural profiles are language, religion, sexual orientation, education, competence, abilities, and familiar structure and other features that only emerge when talking and interacting with the new person. These cultural profiles are the ones that truly disclose who the person is: quality, integrity, intelligence, empathy. Therefore, to appreciate the talent and contribution that the newcomer can make at a professional and social level, it is precisely the right thing to do, not just judge by the first impression. In fact, misjudging is costly and dangerous; it risks losing people of great value at personal and business levels.

Gender

During the past 10 million years of the history of humanity, the role of the male has been that of "hunter" and provider while the female has acted as "caretaker" and administrator of the supplies brought in by the male so that all the members of the tribe or family could live and could last as long as possible. Only in the past one hundred years, women have assumed roles historically reserved for males. It is not a coincidence that women have gradually, rapidly, and actively entered all sectors of the social, economic, technology and governance sectors.

There have been critical times which have triggered this exponential transition.

In New York, March 25, 1911, the suicide of female workers in the Triangle Shirtwaist Co. factory protesting against abusive salary and working conditions fueled the process. In the same way, during the Second World War (1939-1945), women replaced men, in all professional, production, and service activities who were away fighting the world war. In 1995, more women than men in the developed countries had a university degree. The talent pull is in the female population in developed areas of the world. In 2020, Ursula von der Leyen, a woman, was elected president of the European Union, at the same time as Christine Lagarde was named head of the Central European Bank. And in 2022, Roberta Metsola was elected by vast majority president of the European Parliament. Three women in the most powerful positions in the world only one hundred years later, while the Prime Minister of Germany, Angela Merkel retired after fifteen years of heading her country which had been leading European Union growth for the past decades.

Women in underdeveloped areas are leading the entrepreneurial micro business sector launched by Muhammad Yunus, a Bangladeshi social entrepreneur, banker, economist, and civil society leader who was awarded the Nobel Peace Prize for founding the Grameen Bank and pioneering the concepts of microcredit and microfinance. These loans are given to entrepreneurs too poor to qualify for traditional bank loans. Yunus and the Grameen Bank were jointly awarded the Nobel Peace Prize "for their efforts through microcredit to create economic and social development from below." The Norwegian Nobel Committee said that "lasting peace cannot be achieved unless large population groups find ways in which to break out of poverty," and that "across cultures and civilizations, Yunus and Grameen Bank have shown that even the poorest of the poor can work to bring about their own development."

Fifty-two percent of the world population is female. Women decide eighty percent of purchase of products, goods, and services. Today women hold leading positions in service organizations, industry, finances, banking, culture, art, and sports.

This stunning inclusion of women in all sectors of the global scenario coincides with the one hundred years of highest development ever of humanity. Is it a coincidence, or have women propelled this unprecedented progress?

Of the 193 countries in the world, only ten are ruled by women, as described by David Icke in a video that became viral. And these women had the most fortunate behavior in the war against the pandemic. These women have demonstrated different types of behavior from that of men regarding the decision-making process to combat the virus, as well as the time it took them to take action early in 2020. There was a significant difference in the degree of empathy embedded in their early way of acting with the vision that the country and its peoples had to prepare for a better future.

In Germany, Angela Merkel set a battery of actions with which the entire country had to comply. These included selective confinement and guaranteed the salary of workers who lost their jobs. As a result, in January and February 2020 there were ten deaths and 2,035 persons infected in a population of 83 million people.

Sanna Marin, thirty-four years old, president of Finland, also implemented a battery of activities. She asked for help from virtual media "influencers" in order disseminate all the daily recommendations. One hundred and seventy two people died in the first wave, out of a population of six million inhabitants.

Norway, with Erna Solberg as head of government, ordered confinement. She was very creative and addressed a speech only for the children. She explained exactly what was happening and convinced the children of their relevant importance at these moments making them allies to guarantee that all parents follow the instruction given by the government to fight the virus. "In a crisis like this, the children need to feel that they are taken into account." In a country of five million, there were only 194 deaths during the first wave.

In Denmark, Mette Frederiksen reacted in January and carried out obligatory massive tests, confinement, covered seventy percent of the salaries of the workers that lost their jobs, and financed companies which lost their business. The economy was not closed. Only two persons died during the first wave.

On the other hand, in Spain, President Pedro Sanchez did not announce the threat of a pandemic until March 2020 when he informed that he had a telephone meeting with president Xi Jinping of China, complaining about the loss of three million masks that had been bought by the Spanish government from Chinese suppliers. Boris Johnson, Prime Minister of the United Kingdom, ignored the virus until he was seriously infected. Donald Trump, president of the United States mocked the virus, and suggested people use bleach to combat the virus, while the country reported the largest number of deaths worldwide and suffered the largest number of bankruptcies ever.

The OECD identifies the benefits of the empowerment of women in an outstanding research project carried out between 1970 and 2009. As the number of women in the labor market increases, the higher the economy develops in the country. So, the degree of development of a country can be determined by the percentage of women in active in the economy.

The economic empowerment of women is an asset for any country. The companies greatly benefit by putting women in decision making positions, because they increase productivity in the organization. The report states that in a company where three or more women are in upper positions there is a higher level of performance in all aspects of the organization for which they have a higher professional training level. Women are responsible for over fifty percent of the economic growth of countries in the OCDE.

The issue is not to integrate women in any corporate position just because they are women and little less to meet the gender inclusion quantitative objective of the company. The study refers to women with the professional capacities and competencies that require the position which they occupy.

The American University in Cairo – Egypt Women on Boards Observatory is a consortium initiated by the university's School of Business and supports the country's national objective of achieving the presence of thirty percent women in Egyptian companies by 2030. The consortium develops an annual monitoring report, providing a snapshot of female board representation across different categories helping to identify gaps, a database designed to support the placement of women on these boards, a board placement service offered to companies looking to increase female representation, and capacity building and awareness training for both male and female board members.

The companies with women in upper management positions generate a superior gross profit of 47.6%, in comparison to those which have men in the same rankings and positions, according to a research carried out by McKinsey consulting organization in 303 large Latin American companies. The companies with more women in upper management positions are more profitable, according to a study published by the Peterson Institute for International Economics, which researches the impact of gender diversity on companies.

The investigation, which analyzed 21,980 companies in ninety-one countries, demonstrates that the behavior of the companies increases in proportion with the number women in upper leadership positions in the organization. The difference is not small: companies that have at least thirty percent female presence in high executive areas report over fifteen percent higher benefits.

The IESE Business School has been contributing since 1958 to vocational education and management of men and women without any type of distinction. In 1999, Nuria Chinchilla founded the International Center for Work and Family to help address existing barriers in work and family life, and identify ways of leveraging support from public and private institutions that may sponsor the professional inclusion of women who are still responsible for the greater part of family tasks. The IFREI (IESE Family Responsible Employer Index) in more than one country, has helps many thousands of persons and families to improve the conciliation of their professional and family life.

TMB is very active in activities that empower women in leadership:

- Promote women to positions of responsibility.
- Design training for the development of specific capabilities.
- Disseminate the "Women in Movement" video in the intranet, which

illustrates female testimonials that occupy positions which have been historically reserved for men.

- Promote the photograph collection "Femenine Humanism," which gives visibility to the achievement of outstanding women in the history of humanity.
- In collaboration with the Polytechnic University of Catalonia, give visibility of student profiles who have developed professionally in TMB.

Women lead the third sector, key to the present and future sustainable social and economic development. According to the report, "The third social action sector in 2015: impact of a crisis," elaborated by the Social Action of non-for-profit organizations, Platform (POAS) and the Third Sector Platform, report that 78.4% of persons that work in the sector are women. In addition, 51.4% of the directors of these non-for-profit organization are women.

According to the analysis conducted by the OIT (International Work Organization in 2010), women are overrepresented in the health care and communication services sectors, which are well known for the low status and remuneration of their staff.

The gender differences affect the legislation in developing areas of the world. It is very sad to see that ninety percent of the 143 economies studied in the research, register at least one legal difference that hampers the economic opportunities of women.

In the thousands of years of human history, the parents have educated their sons to govern, order, produce, work, and research, while they educated their daughters to find a man to follow and obey with whom build up and take care of the family. The transformation in the role of the woman has happened only over two or three generations, a remarkable change which is not easily assimilated by the parents when it is their turn to educate sons and daughters to work together towards the future.

If the female working population increased at the level of the present situation in Sweden, the Spanish economy would grow by sixteen percent to 257,000 million euros. In 2020, the Women in Work index, developed by PwC, classified thirty-three countries that comply with the OECD, following female integration in its labor markets. The index is based on five large indicators: wage break, female participation in the labor market, difference in participation between men and women in the labor market, self-employed women and women employed full time. Spain occupies the twenty-eight percent place in this ranking.

To help eliminate the gender gap in upper management levels of companies, whether public or private, the W2W program has been launched. The project has successfully trained over 200 professional women to occupy seat in boards of directors of different corporation. The W2W program include four lines of work: academic training in corporate governance, personal development, mentoring with active counselors, experts in corporate governance and headhunter. Sandra Deltell who is responsible in Price Waterhouse-Coopers for diversity projects, reports that forty-five women that have participated in this program are already board members in major Spanish companies or foreign corporations that operate in Spain.

It is not surprising that the prevailing stereotypes create a barrier to full inclusion of women who are highly qualified in professional skills. It is then obvious that a company that does not have women in decision-making positions has a high risk of obsolescence. Its external public, clients, suppliers, and administrations also have a growing number of women in upper management to relate with. The company must have a labor force that reflects the profile of its external publics to ensure its quality permanence in the markets, especially in the case of gender, because women decide eighty percent of the purchase of products, goods, and services.

The new forms of working contribute to this integration. Women need to manage their time with flexibility. Women have fully demonstrated all these years' high levels of commitment to their professional responsibilities. This is a natural process. The time will come when parents educate in equal rights and opportunities both their sons and daughters. Then, there will not be discrimination against women nor men, because the prevailing stereotypes that have conditioned unequal human behavior over ten million years will have vanished.

Age

The transformation in the use of information technology, production and distribution systems directly conditions the capacity of individuals to integrate and optimize these new tools. Yes, the young people who are involved in the organization are more prepared to use new technologies, because they created them. Nevertheless, the senior population of the organizations has irreplaceable value of accumulated experience during all the years of personal and professional involvement in the company and the external business sector in general. The company cannot disregard any of these competencies. "We are looking for elder employees to become the store with more wisdom" is the strategic decision of B&Q, a retail store located in Macclesfield, in the United Kingdom. Its recruitment campaign received 600 qualified requests for the fifty -five jobs opened. The selection was based on matching the current demographic profiles of the store clients. The result was an eighteen percent increase in benefits, a thirty-three percent decrease in absenteeism, a fifty-nine percent decrease in stock losses and six times less rotation when compared with other stores in the area.

That fact that in 2020, the population over sixty-five was going to be larger than the group age under eighteen years old, is something that forecasting reports have been announcing back since back in the late nineties.

This age gap has multiple effects. On the pension system, for instance, which puts the pensions at a risk as there are fewer entrants in the labor market that will not be able to sustain a retired population with a life expectancy that increases by ten hours per day. It does not reflect the reality of the number of elder people who live alone (800,000 in Spain); nor the quality and cost of health care for the members of the community; nor the adequacy of products and services offered to a growing number of consumers who aim at enjoying an active retired lifetime and therefore demand to be treated accordingly. Active seniors make up the largest and fastest growing consumer market. There is an infinite range of opportunities for companies and self-employed workers to service a market of elderly people who have a very different behavioral profile from previous generations that retired.

Intergenerational mentoring is an extremely effective practice for workers and businesses. Those who have lived longer in the company are the ideal mentors for the young employees, not only because they are holders of experience, but also because the seniors feel a renewed sense of belonging which wins them more respect on one hand, and high satisfaction on the other to see that their young mentees advance in the organization. Mentoring the younger employees in the company is also a learning process for the seniors who enlarge a friendly use of technology. Research proves that they start contributing again to corporate development with at a higher rate than before.

Belk College of Business, University of North Carolina at Charlotte develops Inclusive Leadership Science. The institution uses leadership science research to train the next generation of diverse business leaders who can fill the gap that many companies face in achieving their DEIB goals. Led by faculty, George Banks and Janaki Gooty, concepts related to DEI, #MeToo and #BLM are incorporated into classrooms at all levels; the school embraces opportunities to promote the careers of those from underrepresented backgrounds; faculty deliver trainings, talks, and articles across audiences on topics related to DEIB.

Disability

You can analyze the behavior of inclusion in relationships related to the disability profile. The companies are generally resistant when it comes to the integration of persons with disabilities in their workforce, even though the candidate may have a proved record of professional competence for the given task.

If this is the case, it is likely that the rest of the employees will be affected in regard to social inclusion and interpersonal relations with the disabled candidate. The pressure may reduce their personal and professional performance in the job. Frequently employees with some disability have a higher performance in the position. Beethoven was left-handed. Steven Hopkins suffered from ELA, President Franklin D. Roosevelt had paralysis due to infant poliomyelitis. Their disabilities did not prevent them from being outstanding in their position.

In Spain, the Special Centers for Employment was created as a mechanism of employing people with disabilities in the labor market. The center (CEE) creates service units that later subcontract to companies. Such as maintenance, accounting, gardening, manufacturing, printing, etc. The cost of the subcontracted services helps companies meet the legal mandate set by the state called LISMI. Companies with over fifty employees must have at least two percent disabled employees in the payroll. Subcontracting work to CEE justifies the salaries that companies must pay disabled employed even though they are, in this case, external to the organization.

In Brazil, the labor law establishes that companies must have a range between two to five percent of workers with disabilities. On the other hand, in Mexico and the United States there is no such obligation, and it is assumed that the company contracts persons based on their professional competencies regardless of whether they have a disability or not, as long as the person demonstrates high quality performance in the job.

The Nova School of Business & Economics, Universidade Nova of Lisbon promotes the Inclusive Community Forum (ICF) that focuses on increasing the participation of people with disabilities in the workforce and aims to promote a more inclusive community. Through its Peer2Peer program, students work with disabled people looking for work, identifying their capabilities and overcoming barriers.

MRW - (a Spanish transport company), has a firm equity selecting policy. When choosing between candidates with the same high standard professional qualification, the candidate with a disability profile was recruited. Paco Martín Rius, the corporate CEO explains that: "employees with disabilities, who of course had high competence standards, are more efficient, loyal to the organization, are highly committed with their work than abled employees." Martin Rius insists that disabled employees hold a sense of loyalty and belonging that they transmit to the rest of the team. And what is more, he reports that in MRW there is measurable evidence that they are more efficient and creative therefore contributing to raising the productivity standards of the rest of the employees of the department.

The SIFU Group, founded in 1997 by Albert Campabadal Mas, creates work for over than 4500 persons, out of which ninety percent are disabled. The organization operates as a Special Center for Employment with thirty delegations and services contracted with more than 1600 public and private companies from all sectors. Endesa, La Caixa, Iberdrola, INDRA, Mercadona, Media Markt, and Repsol, among other companies, source Grupo Sifu quality professional services. At the same time the company complies with the labor legislation regarding the two percent disabled employees in the workforce.

These are externalized functions carried out with high quality standards. The range of services that the SIFU Group offers to its client companies is very broad: integrated infrastructure management, externalization of auxiliary services, environment services and maintenance. It also offers qualified workers for sectors such as industry, hotels, retail, and manufacturing. Disability does not totally disable a person. On the contrary, people with disabilities tend to be more efficient and demonstrate higher level of loyalty and highly value work. Albert Campabadal, whose commitment with an inclusive and sustainable company is more than evident, is expanding Grupo SIFU internationally and has started operations in France and Andorra.

Four million people, nine percent of the population of Spain, have some type of disability, which means that one in every three families has a person with some type of dysfunction. One point eight million in active working age gap are unemployed, mainly as a result of discriminatory attitudes of members of the business world. In Spain, persons with over thirty-three percent certified disabilities receive a life-long pension according to the level of disability. The average pension is between 200€ and 400€ monthly, which by no means is enough to live on but that members of the community and their parents refuse to give up. Something that can happen is the disabled person works and has income over 11.000€ a year, including the amount of the pension they receive. The result is a great loss of talent in many cases for a country that needs a broad community of workers to support the pension system. And a great loss of opportunity for these persons to develop a personal and professional life according to their education level of competencies.

Language

Sounds were the primitive type of communication used which later developed into languages that the different groups of people around the world used to talk to each other. The idiom is the maximum expression of the culture that identifies a community of people. Its construction, its meaning, and its way of expressing reflect their culture, the way of thinking, the way of talking and the way of living. Currently, there are 7,000 languages spoken by peoples from different countries, as well as a considerable number of dialects. Languages and dialects that branch from seven basic tongues: Mandarin, Castilian, English, Hindi, Arabic, and Russian.

Most citizens of the European Union share the same currency and economic system, but not the same language. The citizens of each member state that joins the European Union keep on using their own language, which traditionally goes back for many centuries. That is not the case of the United States where the entire population speaks English, besides their native parent language.

Not so in India, where English is the language used by the administrations. While the rest of the population speaks 2000 languages and dialects, Hindi is the official national idiom spoken by thirty percent of the population.

In China, Mandarin is obligatory nationwide while local traditional languages or dialects are freely spoken all over the country, which is divided into thirty-four territories, twenty-three provinces, five autonomous regions, and two regions with special administration status.

The one common language policy has been very effective in China and has greatly contributed to the global leadership position the country has conquered in the past forty years. In this respect India is at a disadvantage.

Global communication between an exorbitantly diverse populations is a clear case of global diversity. People today tend to learn different languages in order to be able to interact personally and professionally with persons from other countries and parts of the world. Globalization makes it compulsory to be able to hold quality communications with other peoples and other groups on social, economic, technical, and cultural grounds. Personal and professional sustainability today and in the future depends on intercultural talent and skills, not only on hard knowledge. Technology is contributing to this mega-intercultural dialogue with virtual translations services that are extremely valuable for companies, governments, artists, students, and anyone who needs to keep updated in the major changes the condition their lives.

Ethnicity

The groups of people living in the world today developed from five main ethnic groups: the original Indians or red skins, the Oriental yellow skins, the white-skinned Caucasians, the black-skinned Africans, and the dark-skinned Hindus. Curiosity and the need to find suppliers has set off the mobility of peoples from the beginning of times, particularly in the past twenty centuries when merchants in search of spices, metals, textiles from other parts of the earth which were new and attractive for their land of origin. The conquerors have always aimed at winning over resources, knowledge, and development to have more power. The global socio, economic, and political map of presently 7.57 million people is constantly changing. A world where ten percent of its citizens are white.

The General Directorate for Equal Rights, Ethnic, and Racial Diversity of the Ministry of Equality has opened the debate on the convenience of introducing a structured approach to ethnic origin in the statistics, studies, and surveys of the population in Spain. The convenience of obtaining desegregated statistics regarding ethnic origin for the better-quality formulation of public policies oriented to eliminate ethnic discrimination and promote the inclusion of communities that are more often victims of racial discrimination. The argument is that having more information regarding the gaps in the implementation of actions inadequately applied by public, civil, economic, and cultural groups, to comply with the UN recommendation as well as with the European Union.

The CERD Committee of the UN establishes that this measure is transcendental in order to identify and better protect the ethnic groups present in the territory, reduce the different types of discrimination and trends that work against them, and the consequent need to move forward. Nicolás Marugán Zalba, Deputy Director General of the Equal Treatment and Racial Ethnic Diversity, emphasizes that, "in the European Union, the 2020-2025 anti-racial action plan is a comprehensive and essential information to develop useful public policy, as well as the need to request data related to ethic origin in order to be able to collect all the subjective experiences of both of discrimination and victimism as structural aspects of racism and discrimination."

Nationality of Origin

IOM's World Migration Report Shows Global Displacement Rising Despite COVID-19 mobility. It limits. According to Marie McAuliffe, report editor, IOM has an obligation to demystify the complexity and diversity of human mobility. This is particularly relevant in the areas in which IOM works to provide humanitarian assistance to people who have been displaced, including by weather events, conflict and persecution, or to those who have become stranded during crises, such as COVID-19. The number of international migrants has grown from eighty-four million globally in 1970 to 281 million in 2020, although when global population growth is factored in, the proportion of international migrants has only inched up from 2.3 percent to 3.6 percent of the present world's population. This is a small minority of the world's population, meaning that staying within one's country of birth remains, overwhelmingly, the norm. The great majority of people do not migrate across borders; much larger numbers migrate within countries.

The top ten reasons for migrating movements are: escaping hardship, conflict, and persecution; seeking a better quality of life; displacement because of environmental factors; family reunification; search for professional opportunities; education; following cultures of migration; economic reasons.

This human behavior explains why the vast majority of people prefer to be in their comfort zone and tend to be more and more selective when choosing friends, and professional relations to interrelate easily. Evidently, this personal attitude does not stop the reality of the global diverse population which increasingly brings peoples of all races, beliefs, and languages together.

The National Basketball Association (NBA), for example, announces "today there are 107 international players from forty.one countries on opening-night rosters for the 2020-21 season, including a record seventeen Canadian players and a record-tying fourteen African players. This marks the seventh consecutive season that opening-night rosters feature at least one hundred international players."

This is just an example to prove that it is essential for all types of institutions to introduce diversity awareness programs and inclusive team building in order to manage the differences that are embedded in any type of institution or social group. In the same way, the education system must introduce diversity inclusion as core competences to be introduced since childhood in order to combat unconscious bias behaviors that create conflicts in all areas of activities during the entire lifetime.

The workforce of any company must reflect the demographic profile of their target audience; otherwise, the organization will not be able to attract and retain customers, suppliers or external publics effectively to keep a sustainable position in present and future extremely diverse markets.

It only took two hours for Larry Page, founder of Google, to announce that the company would move out of the United States if the law proposed by President Trump to forbid the entrance of citizens from fourteen countries was approved. "Google services people in 165 countries who use Google owned domains, so the company needs workers from all these countries where it has clients, in order to better understand their needs and preferences and therefor give the best service." The law was not passed.

Language

UNESCO considers culture the set of distinctive spiritual, material, intellectual, and affective traits that identify a society or a social group, which evidently conditions the behavior of each human group that lives in a given geographical area, with the exception of the Roma nation, whose members live in different countries of the world without losing their personality or legal identity. Likewise, the Jewish population, whose members, despite having Israel as their homeland, live and actively participate in all the social, economic, and political activities of the countries where they live. The same occurs with the Muslim world, rapidly spreading across the planet, safeguarding their religious practices and believes. Otherwise, the group of persons that live in a country today tend to share common basic behaviors languages, and interests that characterizes each nation. So, in this case, the Germans live in Germany and the Mexicans in Mexico, which explains the style of life of the people of each country. But when interacting, they differ considerably in their way of working and decision making, which can create conflicts when having personal and professional relationships.

The natives of specific cultures tend to live in a certain geographical area and, although they share the same continent, as in the case of Europe, each country has its own culture. That is, their share a set of principles, priorities, ways of speaking, working and living. The Spanish eat between 13:30hrs and 15:00hrs generally, while the English do so at 12:00hrs. The same relates with working time, schooling, television programs, and sporting events. Citizens with different cultures have different social, family, educational, and gastronomic habits, as well as preferred activities and speak the same languages. Most citizens of the European Union share the same currency and economic system, but not the same language. The citizens of each member state that joins the European Union keep on using their own language which traditionally goes back for many centuries. That is not the case of the United States where the entire population speaks English, besides their native parent language.

Not so in India, where English is the language used by the administrations. While the rest of the population speaks 2000 languages and dialects, Hindi is the official national idiom spoken by thirty percent of the population.

In China, Mandarin is obligatory nationwide while local traditional languages or dialects are freely spoken all over the country, which is divided into thirty-four territories, twenty-three provinces, five autonomous regions and two regions with special administration status.

The one common language policy has been very effective in China and has greatly contributed to the global leadership position the country has attended in the past forty years. In this respect India is at a disadvantage.

In this fully interactive global world, managing differences is a priority so that people and institutions can leverage the traits that distinguish the culture of the people that make up the country.

Sexual Orientation

The American Psychological Association (APA) explains that being homosexual is not a disease and thirty-five years of scientific research prove that it is not related to mental disorders or emotional or social problems. The research carried out studied thirty-seven homosexual and the other heterosexuals; and ten couples who were both gay. Their research reports there are five regions of the genome where the methylation pattern appears very closely linked to sexual orientation. A model that predicted sexual orientation based on these patterns did so with seventy percent accuracy within this group. "This seems to confirm that sexual orientation is a physical characteristic that the person is born with and not a social behavior that should be punished for being different from that of the majority of the population."

Thus, there are organizations that respect and value the sexual identity of their community of people, such as PwC, which in 2014 had established networks of LGTBI employees in four countries that in 2020 had extended to another twenty-one more countries. Now they continue to establish Shine groups, especially in United States.

The sexual orientation of historical homosexuals whose talent and contribution to humanity have always been recognized has been ignored, for example, Socrates, Plato, Aristoteles, Alexander the Great, Julius Caesar, Michelangelo, Leonardo da Vinci, William Shakespeare, Oscar Wilde, Federico García Lorca, or Freddie Mercury (with sales of up to 300 million copies of his records). Homosexual behavior is accepted from prominent people and celebrities and not from co-workers or from acquaintances. This is an unjustified social discrimination that must be abolished, because people have the right to fully live their lives.

In Germany in 2010, the Deutsche Bank launched a service aimed at managing assets of gay persons by a company agent with the same sexual orientation. It was advertised in mass media as well as directly to its entire customer base. The program had an overwhelming success.

Discriminating against homosexuality is mainly the result of religious practices that impose sexual behavior to promote procreation and, therefore, the relationship between two people of the same sex is forbidden. This prejudice has prevailed for centuries. To discriminate against a person because of a different physical condition is a discriminatory practice penalized by the European Union legislation.

CHAPTER 16

Inclusion:
Awareness and Inclusion

The workforce, that is, the community of people that actively contribute to the development of any company or organization, is already diverse, because every person on earth is unique. Different from each other in one way or another. Managing inclusion is a fundamental and constant function of the team in charge of enhancing the human factor in the company.

Regarding new entrants, the organization must act with well-thought dynamic policies in order to integrate these persons as full members of the group as soon as possible. The objective is to establish active policies to develop a career plan within the organization for all employees and to value unlocked skills of new candidates that can be of great advantage to share with colleagues, as well as for the institution. It is a priority to listen and take into account their contributions, their way of analyzing and taking decisions that can introduce new and more effective ways of proceeding in the company. It entails fostering professional inclusion. Thus, as the workforce of the organization grows, so does its capacity to innovate, which will grant sustainable development of the organization.

To achieve this level of inclusion, the company must "give permission" to its people and establish communication channels in both directions; to disseminate training programs, promotion opportunities, social projects and information in general; as well as to encourage staff members to send in ideas and suggestions for projects that could be launched and that would contribute to achieve corporate objectives. These proposals represent a great value because behind them there is a person willing to actively participate in its achievement. All suggestions should be carefully considered to evaluate its possible contribution to corporate range of activities that add value to the brand. And, if approved, allow the employee that presented it to actively participate in rolling out the initiative.

In the research carried out by the IEGD, there is a very significant finding in this regard. Seventy-four percent of the companies affirm that their employees are highly qualified for the function they perform, nevertheless only eleven percent of the companies that operate in Spain are open to the idea that workers should be stimulated to design projects and ways of working. Only twenty-two percent state that they encourage their staff members to express their expertise and opinions freely.

Failure to do so raises barriers to the contribution and initiatives of diverse talented workers and therefore becomes a key factor in potential business loss. Many employees are reluctant to propose new ideas and projects for fear of being segregated for acting "outside of the norm" and losing promotion opportunities. Thus, forty-two percent of employees decide not to propose new ways of doing things, in which case there can be a significant loss of business opportunity.

Nestlé diversifies and expands by selecting and taking over the best "brand" in the countries in which the corporation aims at doing business. Instead, 3M has based its development and leadership policy on formalizing entrepreneurial projects of its workers as a business policy. A great example is Post-it, created by Spencer Silver and an employee in 1968. Silver was trying to develop a self-adhesive glue that pasted permanently. Yet, by mistake, he invented a self-adhesive glue that does not stick permanently or damage paper surface. The product was disregarded. But it was not thrown away, as the company secretaries began to use it to paste notes on folders and files. In view of the success, 3M launched the new product, and the "inventor" has made great profits from a corporate business project. Fiftyyears later, it continues to be a leader in the sector. What everyone at 3M has very clear is that innovation is not only not forbidden in the company; quite the contrary, the company expects all its workers to propose ideas for new products and related business to 3M for diversification and sustainable growth.

Exclusion is the main cause of the costly brain drainage from organizations. To belong is to contribute to the actions of the company; it is to optimize professional time and intelligence dedicated to professional tasks. It deals with enjoying the responsibilities that are carried out and not perceiving them as a workload. This inclusion results in a considerable reduction in absenteeism and turnover, as well as in an increase in the efficient use of time. All critical cost factors for the organization have a critical impact on the corporate bottom line.

Dava Newman is NASA's first Chief Deputy Engineer and had led the Massachusetts Institute of Technology's flagship laboratory since July 2021.

"I plan to start by doing a lot of listening and learning," Newman says. "I like to meet people where they are, and to encourage them to put all their great ideas on the table. I think that's the best way to go forward, working with the whole community — faculty, students and staff — to tap into everyone's creativity. I can't wait to get started. There is so much exciting, important work to do… together."

Newman's unusually broad range of interests combined with disciplinary expertise and talent for invention fit with the Media Lab's approach of combining diverse perspectives to build more productive, equitable, and satisfying societies. In an interview with Esther Paniagua, she affirmed that "excellence is achieved with diversity."

"We want people of all disciplines to go further and transgress them. Diverse people in terms of gender, race, and culture who can bring different visions and a critical look. Do not be afraid. We know that excellence is achieved with diversity. The best ideas come when you invite everyone to join. Having as many perspectives and ideas as possible fuels creativity. This is critical to moving forward, especially when trying to build the future, a better future. My job is to help create inclusive, high-performance teams. We want to make sure that we do not exclude anyone. All visions help us to be the best version of ourselves.

"My current research is related to the development of innovative technologies for advanced exploration missions to the Moon and Mars. We want to be at the forefront and be able to say that our use of AI is ethical, equitable, and capable of providing value to the entire population and not just to a subset of the global citizens. When we use AI do so considering the added value it can bring and how AI can serve society."

As mentioned earlier, the contribution to inclusion technologies that in 2003 Professor Joseph Di Stefano and his team from the University of Lausanne developed is extremely valuable.

Extensive research is an outstanding contribution to the understanding of the factors that have to be taken into consideration in order to build up inclusive behaviors. The Di Stefano team created a very effective tool named MBI (mapping, bridging, and inclusion) a tool that builds up inclusion in groups.

The methodology establishes an informal session in which all participants of the group share information regarding their culture and behaviors with the rest of the team. The objective is for all to really start to know each other, their childhood experiences, their dreams and preferences.

That is, exchanging cultural and behavioral personal experiences draws the cultural map of each team member to really understand the reason that condition their interpersonal relations and decision-making process. The second step is to build bridges between all these personal differences and turn them into values rather than conflict detonators. Then a common shared objective can be set that brings together all the team members. Inclusion on the basis of valuing their differences in then achieved. The result is the high level of performance of the group in generating innovation and efficiency for their own satisfaction and for organizational results.

If inclusion generates innovation, exclusion is a universal mishap that causes conflicts at the political and global levels. Conflicts in the social and economic environments of countries are seriously responsible for the lack of sustainability that currently threatens the balance of humanity. The refusal of other ways of being and of proceeding is at the base of the major global conflicts between leaders and countries. In this globalized world, more than forty terrorist groups caused 14,000 deaths. Currently, twenty-five countries are at war and cause an average of 385,000 deaths a year (reported by UN).

According to WHO, 250,000 children commit suicide each year (seventy percent girls and thirty percent boys), victims of school bulling and family tensions. In Spain, suicide is the second major cause of infant death after health problems. To address this dramatic reality in Madrid, Daniel de Torres organized the IV Anti-Rumor Youth Summit in September 2019. Over fifty young people from different cities participated. The Escape Room methodology was used to fight this living drama which is unfortunately kept silent. Escape Room is a game that combines online and offline tests. Young players learn to respect and include the differences of other youngsters through the tests which they have to answer, using videos, games, characters, and testimonials. Facilitators to this awareness methodology are a core to the effectiveness of the inclusive learning process in order to direct, facilitate, and support working through the game. In other words, to overcome their prejudices towards others.

The instinctive reaction towards people of different profiles and conditions is that of rejection. It is the result of stereotypes acquired in childhood which condition what the person accepts or rejects instinctively (unconscious bias). Preferences that children acquire about what is right or wrong, good or bad, what is accepted or what is rejected, as a result of the behavior of the family, the school and the immediate environment where they live. Therefore, childhood early education is essential to prepare adults to combat discriminatory behaviors. To brilliantly address this issue, Felipe Segovia developed back in the nineties the education system that continues to govern the teaching model of the SEK (San Estanislao de Kostka) international schools.

Its mission is to impart knowledge, skills, commitment, and understanding to enable its students to manage their lives effectively during the rest of the twenty-fist century. In 2000, he founded the Camilo Jose Cela University. The SEK, with his daughter Nieves Segovia Bonet as CEO, has eleven international schools with 5,500 boys and girls between eightand eighteen years of age, of fifty different nationalities. At the Villafranca del Castillo SEK, sessions are facilitated on diversity for the 5th grade children between ten and twelve years old since that course has diversity as its underlying theme throughout the school year. At La Garriga SEK, the 4th grade students study inclusive stories of the "Detectives" to learn that disability does not disable a person for everything.

The detectives of the stories are Tom and Alexandra, a boy in wheelchair and a girl with diction problems who manage to solve all adventures. They are heroes in spite of their disabilities.

Mario Barguño, the author, was born with cerebral palsy and Kelly Arrondes, the designer, is technically blind. Their disabilities have not stopped them from creating amusing tales the children enjoy reading, with an inclusive message. Frequently, the authors attend sessions with the class for the children to learn to value their talent instead of discriminating against them for their disabilities. The program and the sessions are highly valued by the pupils, their parents, and the professors.

Frequently, the members of a group politely ask a new entrant, "do not enter," to avoid conflicts and discomfort. If the group is asked to take in the new person, they act on the premise of, "Come in but we will ignore you." When the new person is definitely going to be part of the team, their position can be that of, "Come in and behave like us." Whereas the right thing to do when a new and different person joins the group is to encourage inclusive behavior towards newcomers: "Come in and we will be a new group." This attitude should be encouraged in whether it is an external or internal incorporation, from another area of the organization, since internal mobility is a powerful tool for generating innovation.

However, in Spain, fifty-six percent of companies are not satisfied with the performance of their work teams. Only fourteen percent have groups established with a person responsible for promoting the integration of all its members. In thirty-one percent of cases, inclusion is fostered in a less formal way. The assumption is that this will naturally be done by the team members themselves without any need to establish support or protocol.

To encourage internal inclusion, there is a key question to clarify and tools that can help the company achieve its goal. John Naisbitt used to recommend: "ask the people" when redesigning strategies to attract and retain talent. To ensure a balance within the group of people in the organization, the first thing to do is to ask those people what kind of support they need so that they can focus attention on their professional tasks, as well as on managing their personal/family life. If this balance is not achieved, there is no satisfaction in professional life, which consequently affects performance; and there is no balance in personal life. The more balances is personal life; the more efficient is the professional contribution to the workplace.

Metaplan is a very effective tool to address this issue. It is a group exercise that starts by reviewing the vision and mission of the company. Why? Because very often not all the employees in the organization know the extent of the activities of the company and little less its contribution, its output makes to the society and the economy.

It is emphasized that the corporate objectives are only achieved if each member of the workforce contributes with their talent and participation to achieve sustained positions in the marketplace. The first part, "What the company should do for the workers." Suggestions collected from the employees attending the seminar on what the company should do to create an inclusive environment that facilitates the quality of work so that all staff members can have a high level of performance. The second part, "What can I do for the company" refers to the personal commitment that each person assumes to contribute to organizational sustainability. Thus, each employee ends the session with a personal action plan.

Air Products used this methodology in its fourteen subsidiaries in the European Union. The key objective was to extend its corporate policy of promoting diversity as an axis to expand the skills and abilities of its workforce. Air Products has a community of professional engineers who guarantee the optimum quality of their products. It was essential to expand this technical wealth to also include skills in customizing services that would help respond to client companies' new needs, whether they were public or private organizations.

Fourteen groups of consultants were established who worked closely with the leaders in each of the fourteen countries where Air Products has operations in continental Europe. Support was given in their language and culture, with full knowledge of local legislations. Customized technical support was given directly to local leaders to assume diversity as an instrument of local corporate management to achieve specific objectives in each subsidiary. Each country´s leadership team designed the local diversity inclusion programs to meet local and corporate objectives. Five hundred and fifty sessions were held, attended each by twenty workers, to include the entire workforce of European companies in this major transformation process. IEGD led the project. The experience was extraordinary, as well the results achieved throughout the three-year project.

The participants suggested the type of work environment they need to improve work performance and personal life (flexible hours, access to promotion, monetary compensation, social benefits, training, etc.) When later they commit to taking actions to improve the organization's results, what they are actually doing is creating their own personal work plan. A process that highlights their contribution and the commitment they acquire. Achievement is evaluated periodically. This methodological sequence can be applied in face-to-face or virtual seminars, in gaming activities that promote teamwork, and in open environments that motivate fellowship through the potent tool which is "learning by playing."

According to a research conducted by the EIMD for a major UK corporation, eighty-eight percent of workers believe they work longer hours than they should, while sixty-eight percent say they work under pressure and surveillance. In addition, seventy-one percent state that they feel overused, and sixty percent that they do not have time to finish their tasks. The result of the research shows that people currently value their time almost over any other consideration and as a result, time management should be key when designing remuneration policies in companies. Establishing flexible hours and distance work, for example, is the key to facilitating work-life balance and optimizing the efficiency of the organization. Major North American corporations have always featured their employee support policies on their web pages, because it is a very effective way to attract the best talent.

According to research conducted by Jesús C. Guillén, director of Escuela con Cerebro, there are key cycles of the brain that range between 90 and 110 minutes to sustain attention. Similar studies show that sustained attention can only be achieved for short periods that do not exceed fifteen minutes. If this is a well-known fact, why can it be assumed that the longer hours someone spends in the office, the higher the performance, and results?

A significant example is the strategy implemented by Angelines Basagoiti in Sodexos food ticket division: a lights-out policy at five in the afternoon. She presented the results at a seminar organized at IESE Business School in Barcelona. She explained that the division had multiplied its volume of business three-fold had achieved a high degree of performance from the staff, and that the members of the workforce showed a higher degree of satisfaction with the new working method, which allowed them to better conciliate their professional and private life. In addition, the employees individually had exceeded their individual objectives in the company. Angelines explains that, at first, the members of the staff thought that the five o'clock time set could certainly give a certain margin to finish ongoing tasks. So, most employees kept on working. To the amazement of all, the lights went off at 5p.m. sharp, leaving many employees in the middle of a computer task. They immediately learned to structure their time throughout the day in order to organize their work more efficiently and complete their tasks before the daily "blackout."

Employees should not be evaluated by the time they spend in the office, but by the contributions they make to the organization. This important cultural change needs to be assumed by both upper management and workers in search of higher results and better quality of life.

CHAPTER 17

Compensation:
When Money is Not Enough

Compensation policies must take into account that people do not necessarily need to be rewarded financially for the work they do in the company. Recognizing the task employees do for the company rather than for the time of presence at the office is the first step towards developing a healthy compensation policy which benefits both the organization as well as its employees.

It means that the task done contributes in a very positive way to the business objectives of the company. It confirms that the employee is a critical component of the organization.

It represents the difference between routine work and participative work.

Schemes should be set to reward performance of all the company workforce that exceeds expectations. Bonuses tied to results is a usual formula. Sabbatical time is another alternative which empowers all the members of the organization and sets an example which others will surely emulate. The message must be designed to prove that upper management recognizes that success, growth, and company benefits depends entirely on the effort and contribution of each one of its persons.

The compensation strategies depend entirely on the philosophy and financial structure of the organization. Compensation can be monetary or non-monetary, as informed in the investigation carried out on the preferences of employees regarding the value of their time. It revealed that forty-seven percent of the workforce preferred to earn less as long as they have more free time. Offering sabbatical time and flexible hours can be very effective forms of remuneration. Communication and visibility are a source of recognition for employees of all levels that must be taken into account when designing compensation policies.

People have more and more expectation regarding their professional life; because people dedicate over sixty percent of daily time to work, and even more when adding time wasted in mobility. People need to make their work a pleasant and constructive part of daily life. In some ways, this adds more value to the company in the achievement of its mission on the one hand, and satisfy their personal preferences and needs on the other. People must have a sense of belonging to the organization. They have preferences such as time to study new subjects or to acquire new competencies; promotion to different areas of the organization; working for some time in other branches and countries where the company has operations; and being part of innovation teams to manage specific projects, both professional and social. But mainly, to recognize that the contribution of each person makes a distinct impact when it comes to results for the organization as a whole.

The economic empowerment of women is also a good business policy from which companies can generate probable unexpected benefit. As the presence of women in leadership positions increases, so does the efficiency of the organization. It is a fact that companies, where three or more women are present in senior executive functions, register a higher degree of performance in all aspects. An excellent example is the case of Mutua Madrileña and Bankinter in Spain.

There is ample evidence that when women are able to fully develop their potential in the labor market, the macroeconomic benefits are significant, as reported by Boileau Loko and Mame Astou Diouf research in 2009 or Dollar and Gatti in 1999. Research reports that in certain regions the per capita GDP losses attributed to gender disparities in the labor market can be of up to twenty-seven percent (Cuberes and Teignier, 2012). If the participation of women in the economy was raised to the current levels of male participation, according to TPFFL, the whole country would benefit: five percent in the United States, nine percent in Japan, twelve percent in the United Arab Emirates, and thirty-four percent in Egypt.

The salary gap in certain companies can reach a thirty percent difference between what women earn and what men earn for the same tasks and responsibility, a major discrimination which is penalized by law in the European Union

PwC has developed an excellent tool to manage this gap, which unfortunately still exists in multiple organizations. This process has several objectives. One is to compensate people for their real value and their contribution to corporate results. The other is to always operate within the legal framework of the state, since discrimination is penalized by law, as in-companies such as Walmart, the US based retainer. Discrimination is not a wise style of conducting business when it comes to compensating its workforce.

Walmart is the largest company in the world, with 3,000 stores and two million employees, eighty percent of whom are women. Its stores are located in rural areas and suburban areas of large cities. In 2001, a group of female employees sued the company for discriminatory practices based on gender, promotion, age, salary gap, cultural styles, and sexual harassment. Had the litigation been won, it would have involved a fine that would have resulted in the closure of the company. On June 20th, 2011, the distribution giant won the lawsuit on the basis that the process was rejected by the US Supreme Court and an agreement was settled with the demanding group. The truth is that neither the United States nor any cities around the country where the company operate can afford to close a project that creates two million jobs and services a significant part of the rural population. The lawsuit acted as a warning for the distribution giant to rethink a new structure for its business model and among other measures, eliminate discrimination gaps that were currently practices.

The tangible value of the workforce is easy to measure by analyzing the impact of the contribution to company results of the actions each employee performs. In order to assess the intangible contribution, evaluation systems that measure the attitude of consumers and external agents in general of the company and its people, should be carried out at least on a yearly basis.

CHAPTER 18

Innovation: Diversity Generates Creativity and Innovation

Innovation is the direct result of the diverse profiles of the members of a team or of an organization. "Only 10% of the ideas are unique to the world each year; the rest is the result of innovation," as John Naisbitt stated in 1978 in his bestseller Megatrends. And he added: "Companies are in the ongoing business of innovation." Innovating must be a constant activity, whether in people management systems, processes, products or services, or in marketing, distribution, logistics, or sales strategies, as well as in the introduction and application of technology, financial systems, or models to create alliances.

The value of Microsoft shares increased by almost six-fold since 2014 (despite the crisis caused by COVID-19) when Satya Nadella, in 2014, took over leadership role of the empire. In his first email, he wrote to the entire staff: "Our industry does not respect tradition, it only respects innovation." Each member of the workforce rapidly understood that proposing innovative tools, projects, and mechanisms was the way to promote and consolidate a position in the corporation.

Innovation is the critical factor to corporate sustainability; in companies of all sizes, as established by King and Anderson (1995), Abernathy and Utterback (1978) and Isaken (2000), among other researchers. Tatli and O. Zbilgin (2000) propose five motors to guarantee sustaining development of creativity and innovation as a mandatory discipline to ensure the presence of the company in the markets: 1) legal compliance; 2) ability to attract talent; 3) retain a diverse workforce; 4) make visible social responsibility programs; and 5) sustain leadership position of the company in the corporate arena.

In the same way as any other corporate strategy, diversity and inclusion management requires measuring and evaluating its results. That is, measuring the contribution that the programs implemented have on the creation of innovation and the impact on corporate results. This information will then condition the budget allocated in projects designed to implant diversity inclusion at all levels of the organization.

Kaplan and Norton (1996) propose the use of the balanced scorecard, if it is the accounting tool that the organization usually uses. Ricardo Breveeld suggests the use of Portfolio Management. The European Institute for Diversity Management proposes the methodology of cost and benefit indicators to calculate the contribution that each diversity project makes to the sustainability of the company.

Demographic trends and legislative pressures, as well as the competitive strength of the market to attract talent and skills, create barriers to minority groups excluded because of cultural stereotypes of the members of the institutions. The question lies not only in what mechanisms to use to develop a diverse workforce, but also mainly in how to handle its inclusion now and into the future.

Mentoring

To this end, it is very effective to establish a mentoring system throughout the organization, regardless its size. The perfect situation is for every employee to have a mentor that can propitiate their social and professional inclusion. The profile of a mentor is that of a person in the organization who is in the position of introducing the mentee to the culture of the organization, to the way in which the people of the company operate, the way of doing, promoting, and logistics when taking action. It is someone who knows how to transmit the limits of the organization and the hierarchy for decision-making, as well as which are the basic norms to respect and the style of innovation development. And primarily to facilitate interpersonal relationship with the rest of the workers of the organization to ensure the social inclusion of all its people.

This does not mean that the objective is to clone people, quite the contrary. It about knowing the basic norms of behavior within the organization, proposing new ideas that can be accepted and valued without creating conflicts. Mentoring programs in organizations reduce turnover, successfully manage diversity issues, and increase the sense of belonging of its people. There are many additional benefits, such as increased productivity of the workforce, improved socio-labor climate, and development of a competent workforce fully identified with the organization. In addition, trans-generational knowledge is the cornerstone for talent retention. Thus, contact between senior and junior workers is encouraged. Seniors contribute the value of the experience acquired through a life of professional activities and at the same time the young mentees transmit their knowledge of information technology and emerging virtual mechanisms. It is a win-win situation which benefits the organization.

Boeing Corporation, the large Chicago-based aircraft company, is famous for the mentoring policy it offered to the entire workforce so that each person has the opportunity to improve their leadership skills and can develop professionally in its highly competitive and global industry.

Caterpillar, on the other hand, has established a trans-generational three years monitoring program between seniors and junior workers in the company with the firm intention of having an entire workforce with the competencies and skills the company needs to meet its present and future goals.

McGraw-Hill has a very effective mentoring program in which ninety-seven percent of the high-level executives participate as part of their daily tasks and functions in the company. At Bain and Company, a consulting firm, each person has a mentor. This strategy is considered the fundament of its diversity inclusion policy. The company has fifty percent of professional life. The mentoring policy has been the foundation of General Electric and people development strategy for over twenty years and has been extended internationally to include its members in subsidiaries around the world, which have managed to integrate the diversity inclusion policies regardless the cultural differences of the host countries.

The project structure establishes that all persons involved in the company or group, whether from external or internal sources, and regardless of their level in the organizational chart, has the support of a professional and social mentor who guides in how to leverage the different technical and cultural aspects of the business. They act on a voluntary basis to encourage mentees to meet colleagues from other departments and establish fluent social communication that contributes to a feeling of belonging to the organization and therefore, to improve the efficiency of the business process.

Mobility

Mobility makes a difference. Moving workers to join other departments or project groups is a very effective way to create a diverse environment within the existing workforce.

For the company workforce to be diverse does not only depend on new talent joining the organization; the company is already diverse in itself, since all its members have different profiles to a lesser or greater degree. Diversity managers only have to mobilize knowledge and contributions to the different areas of the organization to leverage these differences. All it has to do is to move employees from their usual workplace, temporarily or permanently, to another area or project group of the company.

Lucent Technologies (ATT) set out to increase the profile range of its workforce, which had always been essentially made up by engineers. The policy was based on including marketing executives in each project team. The objective was to add to the eminently technical behavior of the engineers a customized service vision of clients and to develop products and tools of great social value.

Assigning temporary tasks to staff members to other groups that are not their usual ones moves people out of the routine. It also stimulates learning on the part of executives that join the group, while the group benefits from new knowledge, vision, and competences of the new entrant to the team.

When returning to his or her usual role, the employee does so with new ideas that can be put into practice in his or her usual workplace and benefit all the other group members. Seventeen percent of companies in Spain orient their workforce so that they are able to take advantage of and benefit from the diverse profiles of their co-workers, while a growing thirty-one percent do so to a lesser degree and let employees find out for themselves the balance, respect, and inclusion of different cultures and points of view that upgrade employees with diverse profiles.

Assigning an executive for a week or year to a different area of the company can be a form of reward, recognition, and compensation at the same time that it is a value added for that person, as well as for the staff of the new subsidiary which is temporarily included.

A tool was developed for a subsidiary of Telefónica Spain, to bust the intercultural competence of the workforce by establishing mobility for a number of executives to subsidiaries in other countries. To this end, a video game was created. A role-playing story which was the story of a trip to India of a group of persons who did not know each other. During the trip, very extreme situations arose. And what was most significant was that the people from whom less initiatives were expected, at the end were the ones who found creative and viable solutions to the challenges that happened during the trip enhancing the entire venture. At the end of the trip, the group agreed to repeat the experience the following year. The virtual session was exercised by 6,000 executives of the company from different areas of the world.

Mobility, whether internal or external, fosters learning, knowledge exchange, and culture, both in the person that moves to a new location as well as to the group or area in which they temporarily participate. Mobility is a management tool; an opportunity that offers new opportunities to people in the company, as well as to get out of the routine of their job and open up to new environments. This transforms the company into a learning organization.

Retention

The employees who leave the company take with them "knowledge," the know-how they have acquired, the interpersonal relationships they have been able to establish and their experience. They take away an enormous value, the equivalent to the investment that the company has made in each person and, therefore, when the person leaves the organization, it suffers a loss which is basic to calculate and measure. A tangible as well as intangible costs the company has had during the time the person has been employed in the company.

Turnover is a very expensive facet of the corporate process. The exodus of talent and experience must be measured to invest in retention policies and avoid this loss.

According to the research done by Gonzalo Sanchez, head of the faculty of economics of the University of Cadiz, twenty-one percent of companies fully agree with the fact that diverse cultures represent an important value for the organization, and at the same time improving behavioral patterns and other levels of efficiency. On the other hand, eighteen percent protocols their knowledge generation ability to enhance the different areas of the organization and avoid the loss of this know-how. Retaining talent is a key function of the company whose operational responsibility lies in the management of people. But the truth is that it is the responsibility of all members of the institution. An inclusive company is an interesting, productive, stimulating place to work in and for a physical or virtual place where the person enjoys being, belonging, acting, and who find it is positive to dedicate the time and passion.

Siemens established a very important program in Italy aimed at ensuring the quality of life of its engineers at a time when the headquarters were relocated. The main measurement criterion for this operation was the loss of business opportunity for each engineer who left the company as a consequence of this corporate site transfer. The company calculated that it could not afford to lose over twenty percent of its engineers, because their individual replacement cost was equivalent to a year and a half of salary plus the cost of infrastructure. "I can lose a person, but not its experience," was the principle established by the Siemens project leader.

Many companies create clubs or associations for employees who retire or who voluntarily leaves the company for personal reasons. These clubs or associations organize conferences, training, cultural activities, participation in social projects of the company, always establishing mechanisms that extend their "active" life in the organization to the former workers who choose to belong to this organization. TMB, the Barcelona Metropolitan Transport system, for example, has a club of retirees who actively participate in many projects of the organization. Other companies enter into an advisory agreement with former employees who want to remain professionally active, such as Deutsche Bank in Germany. Some companies replace temporary leaves with former workers which is far more efficient, since former workers know the company and therefore replace the employees on leave more effectively and with less margin of error.

Companies that practice these policies convey credibility and a sense of belonging to their entire workforce. Retaining the talent and experience of people who leave the organization is a "business case," an economic and social corporate behavior that contributes to business sustainability.

CHAPTER 19

Time is a Resource:
Personal Treasured Value

Time is no longer a standard measurement unit in this new era, it has become an extremely valuable strategic tool, a resource to evaluate each person for their contribution to the results of the organization, not for the amount of time (hours) of presence in the company. Spain is the country in Europe where people sleep less hours, where they spend more hours at work, and where productivity is lower, forty-ninth place in the productivity international ranking. In research carried out for a British corporation by IEGD, the findings were stunning. Eighty-eight percent of workers believe they work longer hours than they should, while sixty-eight percent say they work under pressure and surveillance. In addition, seventy-two percent state that they feel used, while sixty percent state that they do not have time to finish their tasks.

A multinational company must consider how to improve the performance of its decision makers and senior executives responsible to guaranty the sustainable position of the organization in the domestic market as well as in the global scenario based on its ability to build an inclusive workforce. The same applies to SMEs, although in a more manageable dimension. The research also revealed results that have forced major transformations in the structure of corporate decision-making level. Forty-three percent of workers would be willing to earn less in exchange for more free time. It is particularly interesting that seventy-eight percent of men versus forty-five percent of women declare this preference. Even more significant is that forty-six percent of executives want to reduce their working time, while seventy-seven percent as a preferred way of working. Most significant is that eighty seven percent life out of the office. The argument given by this very exclusive group is that major decisions are generally not made in offices, but they are generally negotiated and taken in meetings outside of the office. They also highlight that their presence in the company can cause significant loss of time due to interruptions, extended interviews, unnecessary meetings, and unexpected calls and visits that do not add value to their work or to the organization. This very select group of corporate leaders point out that waste of their time is extremely costly to the organization. Distractions are a costly result of their physical presence in the company.

This cost of time lost and time wasted, depending on the type of company, can amount to forty percent of the corporate labor, which obviously represents a level of inefficiency that no organization can afford. Therefore, it is then compulsory that personal individual time management is encouraged. Measuring and evaluating the contribution employees make to company objectives from their position in the organizational structure must be evaluated on the basis of performance and not by the time present in the office.

Distance working, which has been enforced by the pandemic to keep up the economic activity of the country, will stay and become the most preferred and dominant way of working towards the future. Efficiency as a whole will improve and in the social arena, demographic curve in developed countries will improve as parents have more time to care for the family.

Nestlé, a wise Swiss company, under the global leadership of José Daniel Gubert as head of human resources, established back in the eighties a flexible labor calendar for all workers of the organization. A two hours arrival time in the morning and another two flexible hours to end the working day was established. The compulsory presence was set for four hours during the working day. This facilitated setting meetings and interaction between all the members of the workforce, as well as complying with personal responsibilities without creating personal or professional tension.

CHAPTER 20

Artificial Intelligence:
Helps and Substitutes Humanity

Artificial intelligence replaces the person in the workplace as derivative of the increased repetitive, cognitive, and complex automation processes. This translates into less need for workers in industrial production, while the demand increases for talent in sectors such as services, and information and technology, among others. This can create unequal job opportunities.

Replacing people in non-receptivity jobs requires the development of diverse professional skills and abilities in new areas of knowledge to promote a sustained working environment in the future. Companies need to count on the type of talent available that will allow them to maintain a competitive position in new markets. The Fourth Industrial Revolution has created a new socio-economic system, according to the report published PwC.

The ethical and responsible use of AI requires three basic elements: the use of large volumes of data, the use of algorithms to act and take decisions, and the gradual reduction of human intervention in any type of process. Some examples of artificial intelligence project which are already operational, and which have limitless applications are:

- In the world today, DNV GL uses wind energy for the use of computers with learning capabilities.
- In the world today, Planet Watcher has the ability to monitor landscapes and safeguard forests to prevent climate disasters.
- In the world today, NASA uses robots to detect pollution, water temperature level, protect phytoplankton with the use of satellite vigilance and learning systems computers.
- In the world today, AirVisual, IBM and Microsoft develop tools to forecast air quality in cities like Beijing.
- In the world today, the UK Met Office and NASA, as well as private sec-

tor companies such as IBM and Microsoft, use AI and self-learning computers to enhance the performance and effectiveness of climate models.

- In the world today, Google reduces energy use by 40% using Deep Mind allegorists, while from Brazil to the Philippines smart systems are used to manage the explosive growth of cities.
- In the world today, the US National Science Foundation EarthCube initiative already employs self-learning computers and 3D simulation.
- In the world today, Planeta has already placed 180 microsatellites in orbit to visualize the entire planet in real time.
- The Fourth Industrial Revolution eliminates rigid infrastructures to move towards agile systems that do not leave environmental footprints.

Artificial intelligence is a great ally for companies and individuals looking for more profitability through escalated productivity that increases consumption due to increased personalization, product design, and marketing. The opportunity to harness AI for the benefit of humanity and its environment is substantial. The intelligence and productivity that are gained by the use of AI can open an infinite variety of solutions to the threatening diverse challenges that humanity presently has: climate change, biodiversity, health of the oceans, water management, environmental pollution, labor, and business efficiency, etc.

Today and in the future, it is necessary to develop knowledge that guarantees an active presence both in the business world and in personal professional development. The difference is that technical training is no longer enough; cultural training will make a difference: empathy, inclusion, multiculturalism, communications, services, the capacity to manage change and flexibility, the vision to detect new needs of a growing diverse costumer population, the ability to detect opportunities in highly vulnerable scenarios, and: the skill to generate constant innovation in order to maintain sustainability in both local and global environments.

Basically, the success of the implementation of AI goes through a humanization process. This will require collaboration between scientists and humanists to ensure that AI permeates efficiently in all productive sectors. Celine Herweijer and Dominic Waughray clearly establish in the report, The Fourth Industrial Revolution for the Earth that, "each agent in the environment is responsible for putting in place the actions that tend to enable humanity to enjoy a sustainable Earth with quality of life in the next decades." The report establishes that humanity already has the tool that can help the sustainability of the Earth: artificial intelligence. It must consolidate.

Companies must establish a committee that manages the use of artificial intelligence to guarantee its implementation with security, ethics, values, and governance, while optimizing the results and managing the risks of the scenario. Pioneering companies that leverage the value of AI to innovate will succeed, as Microsoft has already done with its "AI for Earth" program, which offers tools to universities and administrations working in environmental, business, and social fields to ensure holistic global sustainability. The use of AI systems creates interdisciplinary models which establish new and diverse relationship between industries, trade groups, large technology companies, administrations, legal institutions, non-profit organizations to optimize results and new leverage new solutions.

Given the power of society, it is essential to develop governance structures that are responsive to the diverse cultures and lifestyles that conform to the transformation of humanity towards the future. Artificial intelligence is called upon to support inclusive initiatives for the United Nations Sustainable Development Goals, making investment in D&I a top priority. Artificial intelligence has changed the world forever, and people and their institutions must develop new and different competencies and skills in order to operate in highly diverse future scenarios.

CHAPTER 21

Different Ways of Working: Results Versus Presence

It is not a coincidence that in 2019, as unprecedented crisis has unleashed its effects in every sector of the global scenario. As mentioned earlier, the pandemic has been just one more drop in the deep unbalance in which humanity is immersed. An exorbitant demographic curve where ninety-five percent of growth comes from underdeveloped areas, an economic gap that generates a growing number of millionaires and at the same time massive and increasing numbers of more poor people, a debt of over 120% of the IGP of regions and countries, as well as of companies that frequently cannot even pay the interest, as well as an irresponsible aggression to the climate that endangers the health of the planet.

And the pandemic came to slap and make humanity react. But in the process the health of the world population has been attacked. It will take years to develop immunological treatments to safeguard the people from all over the world from this virus and its mutations.

And if COVID-19 were not enough, Putin invaded Ukraine with a vast number of objectives and side effects besides the horror of devastating a free nation and its people. These includes access to the sea, rebuilding the frontiers of the former USSR, testing all kinds of weapons, creating an energy chaos that weakens the development of the European Union, and redesigning a new global power balance between Russia, China the United States, and the European Union underestimating India.

Men and women in this era have much to change if they want to attain a sustainable high quality of life for all human race in a globalized world. In managing global inequalities, it is necessary to remember that anything that happens in a corner of the world will have an impact in other parts of the world in one way or another, and ultimately cause an impact at global level.

Just to remember The Flight of the Butterfly, a theory developed by José Luis de la Rica that now is very useful to help people understand the evolution of which they are part of, particularly in face of major crises as those the entire world population is living since 2019. It is time to learn, but mainly to prepare to build the new post-virus and post Ukraine era. Only with new skills and abilities and the help of Artificial Intelligence will countries and organizations build sustainable development, innovate in resources, behavior, and systems that can provide a social and economic balance to manage the gaps which are growing in the scenario as a result of these major global crisis. This crisis brings risks but also opportunities. In any case, it forces people and institutions to innovate in new ways of governance, of doing business, of living, and of course of working.

Work is a key factor of human development. Understanding that "work" is an activity carried out by people to obtain an income that can cover their way of living and that of their family. Then the question is: how many people in the world dedicate most of their daily hours to tasks to simply earn the money they need to cover their living expenses and that of their family? Tasks that more than frequently they do not enjoy doing?

This does not contribute to achieve the quality of life to which more people aspired. Time must be dedicated to those activities that the person has a preference for and therefore enjoy most of the hours of the day dedicated to work. Then the employee makes a valuable contribution to corporate efficiency.

If working always involves mobility to a workplace, then it is obvious that the person cannot take care of personal or family needs, and this lack of time is the great cause of the "0" birth rate in areas of the world with industrial and economic development. Although companies hold a commitment to offer conciliation programs in order to contribute to quality of life and to retain their employees, other working schemes can be implemented that allow people to manage their time and be able to comply with their work, personal, and professional commitments, and at the same time contribute to improving the bottom line of the company in which they work, as a result of a higher personal satisfaction for the task they do responding to more effective peoples management policies.

Distance Work

As mentioned earlier, COVID-19 forced managers in organizations to establish distance-working schemes, as well as accelerated the use of AI tools in order to carry out all the corporate process with the added difficulty of stopping the mobility of their employees to comply with the restrictions imposed by governments all over the world. The technology allows all intellectual work to be carried out remotely, from a workstation at the home of the employees or from mobile working units elsewhere. Only repetitive tasks in production requires the presence of the workers in the company plants. And these tasks are being taken over more and more frequently by robots. Not only can robots replace workers in repetitive tasks, but they also do it eliminating human error, which therefore makes the production line far more efficient.

The virus not only forces distance working, but also represents a unique opportunity for those who manage companies and institutions to learn that distance working is much more efficient for the organization. There are three basic reasons:

a) The cost of infrastructure is very high: space, services, energy, maintenance, taxes, insurance. It is imperative that companies calculate the direct impact of each person of the workforce on infrastructure costs. There are countries where the organization´s leader wants to see all members of the staff in the office because they believe that if they stay longer hours more work will be done. Many workers comply with these longer hours hoping to have better opportunities of promotion. The question is whether the company remunerates its workforce by the hours of presence or for achieving defined and measurable objectives with their performance. It is a cultural issue of decision makers who have a high resistance to change and want to perpetuate traditional ways of working. This is the case in Spain not so in the United States where distance work is a usual practice.

b) The person performs more and with greater satisfaction when managing their time; that is, when harmonizing personal and professional commitments efficiently and at the lowest possible cost. The work and family programs are not necessary because the person takes care by setting time schedules that meet the needs both of the professional deliverable, and of family and personal life tasks.

It was compulsory to take advantage of the occasion which acted as a "pilot" in the development of new forms of efficient work for the organization: reducing operating costs, increasing people's productivity and drastically impacting on caring for the environment by reducing mobility of a large part of the working population. Raquel Diaz Caro, human resource manager of Transportes Metropolitans de Barcelona explains that the company saw the number of transport daily users drop by fifty percent while its infrastructure costs remained the same during the pandemic.

Measuring and identifying quantitative indicators that can quantify savings in infrastructure is essential, especially when the "pilot" has proved that it is not necessary to house all workers in the company offices. Equally important are the intangible indicators that measure the performance of workers in the functions they perform, cultural indicators that measure the degree of satisfaction of customers and suppliers, as well as that of the employees of the company themselves, to meet their professional objectives at the same time that they harmonize personal life and family. It is also important to measure the degree of employee satisfaction, the sense of belonging to the organization, the value of the time dedicated to professional tasks, and the reduction in turnover. All indicators that reveal the measurable degree of effectiveness of distance work

Distance working will remain a corporate policy in the future. Nevertheless, distance working must be a voluntary choice of the employee. In March 2021, fifty-two percent of people who work from home in Spain preferred to continue working in this way in order to respond to the historical demands of the working population of having more personal free time, something that the statistic report featured. On the other hand, a very high quality of training is needed, both for workers and for coordinators of work groups.

An excellent example is the methodology which Xerox put in place with distance working personnel to deliver customer service. In 2000, Richard Thomas, the corporate CEO announced during a congress organized by the magazine, Working Woman, the project and its results.

The company offered its entire community of people the opportunity to participate in a distance working program for Customer Service. Joining this project was voluntary. All employees joining the program went through intense training sessions to develop expertise in company products and services on one hand, and to learn how to interact with a group which has a leader to coordinate and meet group targets on the other. The group members agreed on the time each dedicates to the project, as they could later reincorporate to their usual position in the area of the corporation from which they came. The company set up a workstation at the home of each employee, and it was mandatory to maintain the level of communication agreed with the team coordinator to receive requests for services from clients, schedule their visit agendas, and report the results. Each group member committed to the amount number of clients each would service plus reporting and other professional tasks required by the project. The team met at the company office once a week to exchange experiences, recycle product knowledge, and improve service techniques and logistics. Xerox multiplied by three its client service business volume, reached ninety-seven percent satisfaction of the employees participating in the project and drastically reduced infrastructure costs. Xerox saved the cost of office space for the 3,000 employees who at that time had joined the program. She also disclosed that the profile of the staff that had voluntarily joined the project was highly diverse and that it had attracted the best talent of the company.

Employees, for different reasons, needed to have time off that would allow them to develop professional or personal projects, such as training in new technologies, caring of specific needs of the family, and other. This was the case of a young employee who asked to join the program in order to train for the Olympic Games. Also, Leslei Sabo, who temporarily left her position in the commercial department to join the project while raising her three children, later returned to a higher position in the same commercial area. Well-designed distance working is a very powerful business case.

Twitter is leading a gigantic transformation in the corporate world of America. Its president, Anton Andryeyev, ran for two years a company of 3,638 employees with a turnover of 2,210 million dollars and 521,000,000 in profits from his 2,000m2 home in Kauai, on the island of Hawaii. As reported by Elizabeth Dwoskin, the Twitter experience, which empowers and encourages its executives to work from home or from wherever they want, is an example for the rest of the corporate world that can be learned and emulated. It is a profound transformation of work that Andryeyev considers essential for professionals and entrepreneurs to know how to act and leverage the new scenario that emerges with the Fourth Industrial Revolution, which has already begun, and which will be the new way of living and working in the future.

However, Twitter has not closed its offices, as they are a meeting place for employees, teams, and permanent services. Much of its old offices are already for rent as side business for the company, which has gigantic consequences in the real estate sector. Part of company spaces must find other uses, which represents an opportunity for the organization to develop a parallel economic activity, as well as for the real estate sector in general, which will see large spaces available that will impact space renting costs and sales value.

Homes will need to have workspaces, which will also need to redesign their decoration to include workspace. IKEA did not take long to launch the closet / office to respond to the requirements of the growing working population who have become home-based. The challenge was to give a solution to employees who live in small apartments to comfortably carry out their tasks efficiently working from home while living in a small apartment and thus being able to comfortably have their workplace.

Coral Hotels de Canarias has launched a co-living offer to professionals to live and work in a full-service comfortable habitat by the sea. The seven Coral hotels in Tenerife and Fuerteventura are overbooked, while neighboring hotels have closed. They promote long stays to for distance workers from all over the world who chose the climate and location of the Canary Islands as a preferred place to live. The Coral Hotels' motto, which has been overwhelmingly successful, is: "Work from paradise." They have the clear objective of turning their clients into stable residents as the Los Olivos Beach Resort hotel in Tenerife has done.

The American corporate world will telecommute as an unquestionable way of life in the Fourth Industrial Revolution.

Job Sharing

Who says that everyone wants to work a full eight hours a day? There is a vast majority of women and men who want to work fewer hours in the morning, afternoon or nights. Why are trade unions, governments, and managers then trying to impose the archaic eight hours a day format? This working calendar was surely a conquest for the workers in pre-industrial era, but certainly not now in a service and technology driven economy. Trade unions should be alerted that they are no longer defending the true interests of workers today, much less of those in the future.

The British Ministry of Defense has Caroline Pusey and Heather McNaughton directing its 120 subordinates from Monday to Friday under a share-working scheme, as reported by Lopetegui from El País journal. Pusey and McNaughton are equally responsible for their roles. Time, salary, and duties are allocated to ensure quality of performance. "We want to advance in our careers, but we also want to give our children the time they need," explains Pusey.

For more than thirty years, job sharing, and part-time work have been very popular collaborative work formulas in the United States and other developed countries, where people are valued for their performance and not for the time of presence in the company. Since the eighties, companies have embraced diversity policies to improve the effectiveness of organizations, offering all staff, regardless of their diverse profiles, a flexible schedule that allows combining all the professional, family, and personal functions with a high degree of satisfaction.

Switzerland, the United Kingdom, Germany, and Australia are countries in which sharing work has become a relatively frequent formula. In Spain, the trade unions are a barrier to these working modules. The trade unions continue to demand higher wages, more vacation days and more full-time contracts, regardless the fact that today the main preference of people in to manage their own time in order to harmonize professional and personal lives. When people are given permission to manage their own time in a responsible manner, the result is a workforce with a high degree of satisfaction and a high degree of professional efficiency in fulfilling their role in the organization with a deep sense of belonging.

A major advantage of the job-sharing model is that the task has two thinking heads that generally solve problems more effectively at critical moments. As both persons admit, they do not completely disconnect from their areas of responsibility and clients appreciate it, because they have two professionals instead of one that look after their business.

Part-time Work

In the case of part-time schemes, employees are assigned modules of concerted time schedules. For example, in a ten-hour schedule, one worker covers five hours and another the remaining five. This method can apply essentially in production tasks where the type of work is repetitive, facilitating change of personnel without losing process efficacy.

Organizing working times in the company is enriching for everyone. Many people cannot dedicate all of the day to work and need part-time arrangements. A clear result of the research of workers satisfaction was conducted by the EIMD. What decision makers need is to know is that these different working time models represent a benefit to the company. They are not set to solve personal problems of certain profiles of workers. They become a norm of the company which has a high impact on bottom line at the same time it generates satisfaction of the employees.

On the other hand, businesses such as hotels and retail establishments need the presence of workers at specific times throughout the day and week. This forces them to have a large part of their workforce part-time to be able to provide the service that is essential for the organization in specific hours of the day when there are more clients visiting the store, for example. In these cases, it is not cost effective to have more workers required at times when there are less clients in the establishment. In Spain, a service economy, 34.5% of the 19.2 million contracts that were signed between January and November 2018 have been part-time, a faithful reflection of the flexibility that the structure of the service economy in Spain requires.

As published by the Expansion daily newspaper, the Prefabricates Pujal' group located in Mollerussa, Lleida, found a creative solution to the problem of excess supply of employment in the area for the development of its agricultural products sector. The policy was set to attract immigrant male workers to live in the area, rather than come for several weeks at a time along the year. That opened an entire range of female workers.

(their wives) whom the company hired on part-time basis for the new plants they set up of construction materials. This guaranteed a stable and highly satisfied workforce in the nineties. In 2019, the group had registered a capital of 68,919,643 euros and sales of 71,446,796 euros.

The services sector represented 67.2% of IGP in 2008 and was responsible for the creation of 75.6% of new jobs, according to Miguel Cardoso, an economist at BBVA bank. The tourist service sector is essentially seasonal, which forces the corporate world to adapt its structural costs (including, of course, all types of contracts to cover the necessary needs) to hire talent in the months and times of greatest number of tourists. These companies then change the shift the contracts to permanent in order to be able to have the human capital available in times of full occupation.

The hotel sector in Cancun has been outsourcing its workers from the CROC (Revolutionary Confederation of Workers and Peasants. Another system of flexible contracts. As declared by Maria Luisa Alcalde the Quintana Roo Hotel for example, has 802 employees and only two are on the company payroll. This system is fading out due to recent legislation and hotels are hiring the personnel that has been working in the companies for years without knowing that they were on outsourcing conditions before.

The tourism sector is especially vulnerable anywhere in the world in the case of the pandemic, due to the lack of mobility of visitors from other countries, in addition to isolation of the local population. Hotels must change their mindset to understand that they are not in the tourism business, but rather in the business of housing people who need spaces to live, or work, to study, or for healthcare reasons, among other circumstances that require space to rent. Therefore, they can create attractive offers to accommodation that live along. In Spain the market is of 4.8 million people. Or they can create quarters for education centers that need more space for students of which there are already 400 in Spain and growing. Or job-sharing centers. In the UK, for example, there are 122 employees on job-sharing status. Or they may attempt to accommodate the health sector in bad need of beds which has been devastating during the pandemic all over the world. Or house professionals who distance work and prefer to live in the south of Europe rather than in their country of origin.

For example, the Los Olivos Beach Resort hotel (Adeje, Tenerife) is a hotel complex that promotes long stays to distance workers from other parts of the world. This new co-working scheme includes discount package for distance workers with the clear objective of converting its clients into stable residents.

According to La Actualidad, daily newspaper, the trends in new and diverse work schemes emerge as a response to multiple factors: the need for greater flexibility and freedom in office-related decisions, the growing proportion of millennial workers and the need to work in groups to compete and survive in an emerging market. Hotels could leverage this major shift and diversify their business into sustainable formulas of multiple offers.

Networking

The increasing number of organizations that use the networking model for their commercial activities capitalizes on the value that people give to their own personal time. These companies trust the capacity to attract potential distributors by creating a very attractive offer. That is, to offer people the opportunity to create "their own businesses," to become entrepreneurs or businessmen and women-life they learn how to develop their own commercial networks within the corporate structure. There are very diverse styles of business network management.

Amway is the world's largest direct marketing company, created in 1959 in the United States by Jay Van Andel and Richard DeVos to sell a range of products manufactured by their company, as well as products from major brands with which it created alliances to distribute through AMWAY channel, with three million independent distributors, who in turn have their own sales networks.

In 1896, McConnell built a small laboratory in Suffern, New York, which would later become Avon Suffern Research and Development Company. Thus was Avon Products born. McConnell recruited women as agents to introduce cosmetic products to friends and relatives. Avon currently has forty million representatives and operates in 139 countries. Its sales amount to $5.7 billion and it is the world leader in direct sales of cosmetics products. AVON makes a considerable contribution to funding research for the cure of breast cancer which is widely recognized by distributors and clients.

In 1938, Earl Silas Tupper started a plastics manufacturing company, Tupperware Plastics Company. These products sold through traditional channels until, in 1958, Brownie Wise convinced Mr. Tupper to switch to a party plan, a direct marketing system for the product line. Dart Industries was founded to manufacture and market the Tupperware products. In 2018, the network had 3.1 million distributors worldwide, and declared sales of $2.07 billion in 2018. This is the Tupperware corporate statement: "We leverage the diversity of our workers and the growth of opportunities for our sales force around the world. Our business strategy and social investments are oriented to instruct, educate and strengthen women and young people, to develop successfully, who have a key role in the society to which they belong. We provide the tools to our sales force, of 3.1 million people around the world, so that they can provide sustainable solutions that help improve their quality of life, that of their families and their community."

Direct marketing companies have provided the opportunity for millions of women since the 1960s to pursue careers when few had any professional training. Their obsession and goal as they started eighty years ago was to be able send both their sons and daughter to university. Direct marketing companies triggered the process of empowering women until in 1995 more university women than men held university degrees in the European Union. Other companies that operate in networks and incorporate men into their marketing channels are: Stanhome, home care products; ACN, telecommunications, security systems, personal care and well-being; AKEO, healthcare and technology; Captain Tortue, women's ware; Christian Lay, jewelry, costume jewelry, accessories and cosmetics; Mary Kay, beauty and personal care; One Telecom, consultants in telecommunications and Thermomix, kitchen ware. The key to the success of these companies lies in the cost structure and compensation policies destined to their sales network, which can reach sixty-five percent of retail price.

It is important to mention that pyramid companies are not recognized as direct marketing companies; they are fraudulent. The pyramid usually ends in bankruptcy when members of the network can no longer sell to more persons the right to join the organization.

Those looking at the opportunity joining as entrepreneurs direct marketing organizations should be vigilant and join a company with globally recognized success curriculum and never a pyramidal organization.

As technology transforms the scenario bringing obsolescence to the competences and skills acquired on a daily basis; as crises explode in different parts of the world as a result of personal ambitions that put entire populations under desperate conditions; as the health of the climate alters basic living conditions; as globalization shrinks the world and brings together peoples of very diverse profiles and circumstances of very different natures, it is mandatory for people to constantly reinvent the way to live and work with a positive mindset.

CHAPTER 22

Empowering Difference: Diversity Generates Efficiency and Innovation

Those who work in any type of institution are aware that achieving high levels of performance require addressing specific requirements of the workforce. These requirements are as diverse as the profiles of the people who compose the workforce of the organization. It is therefore necessary to look for the common needs of the majority of its agents and create an inclusive environment that allows the entire group to perform with maximum efficiency, to reach common personal goals. Knowing the professional projection of the workforce is an extremely valuable information for the person responsible for3 human resource and diversity corporate management. This x-ray will allow them to design personalized career plans with the objective of retaining those talents which will better contribute to corporate objectives.

Nuria Chinchilla, from the Carmina Roca and Rafael Pich-Aguilera Foundation, chairs the Women and Leadership project at the IESE Business School. The Foundation is very aware of the unique value that women offer and of the barriers they have to override. On their way to leadership positions, they must exceed in order to break the "glass ceilings." The Board-Bound Women program, whether in presence or online format, enjoys a 95 NPS net promotion score as a result of its transformation effect in preparing women for those positions. The project has also gained recognitions in the I-WILL Index (IESE Women in Leadership), which rates the three-four OECD countries in order of relevance as far as female leadership is concerned. It has advanced from two percent of the seats held by women in IBEX boards, to the thirty-two percent.

A way to collect ideas, suggestions, and concerns from all the members of the workforce is to establish information centers where all employees are encouraged to send in their proposals. The proposals are a very valuable source of innovation, at the same time that they reduce conflicts and loss of talent. For example, having the sense of belonging to a company that carriers out socially oriented projects that favor discriminated sectors of the population transmits a high degree of compliance to the working population.

Provital is a fine chemical company established in Barberá del Vallés (Barcelona), with subsidiaries in France, Poland, Brazil, Mexico, the United States, and China, essentially serving the global cosmetic industry. It sponsors the non-profit association Artistas Diversos, which promotes the social and professional inclusion of artists with disabilities. Every two years, it organizes an art contest that awards paintings of artists with disabilities inspired by nature and beauty. All the corporate staff from all subsidiaries vote to select twenty-five finalists. The employees hold ownership of the project. In 2021, 246 works were received from 185 artists. The pre-selection took three weeks during which the employees from different areas met and exchanged their preferences, then chose the paintings that would later decorate the company offices. A professional jury then selects the six award winners. The winning paintings decorate the offices of the company while the employees are welcomed to suggest which paintings they prefer to be near their personal work areas.

The awards ceremony coincides with the opening day of the exhibition of the twenty-five finalist paintings. The event takes place at the Barberá del Vallés City Council. Local personalities attend, as well as delegates from civic associations and residents in general. During the two weeks of the exhibition, inclusive workshops are held for children from all municipal schools to make them aware of the fact that disability does not disable a person for everything, and thus contributes to developing inclusive attitudes since early education. The company measures and evaluates the contribution of the project to corporate results.

The indicators used are the level of interpersonal communications and the degree of improvement (quality and time) of in-company process. In addition, upper management is aware that this is a program that its staff is proud of and looks forward to every second year.

In Mexico, Provital runs a very special project to back up a group of women in agriculture that harvests botanical raw material which the company includes in its product catalogue. This occurs with a similar degree of social and professional involvement and success both from the local organization and its clients.

Implementing projects that support the professional development of the entire workforce not only favors performance in the organization, but also impacts results. Aspects such as life-long learning, exchanges between the different areas of the company at a national and international level, tutoring and mentoring to raise and update the intelligence of the entire organization to turn it into a discrimination free and inclusive environment where all employees feel valued for the differences they bring to the organization.

Twenty-two percent of companies in Spain state that the work environment is one of fellowship in the workplace, while thirty percent attribute it to the existing mechanisms established by the organization to mediate in moments of conflicts that derive essentially from cultural differences (level of education, skills, abilities, languages) and demographic profiles (gender, disability, age, nationality of origin, ethnicity and others) of the members of the workforce.

The aim is to build a space where it is possible to perform tasks as efficiently as possible thanks to up-to-date tools. An environment that rewards trust and respect among co-workers, who know that they can depend on each other to form an excellent team. A supportive scenario that values the times of each person and equally rewards their results. Activities that create an inclusive environment for male and female employees and enrich their workplace. These programs include schemes of flexible time, distance work, interest groups, innovation and creativity, resource networks, awareness, introducing new technologies, training in inter-culturality and new skills, career plan, trans generational mentoring, coaching, evaluating by results, entrepreneurial projects, early retirement assessment, internal mobility, international mobility, participation in social responsibility projects, representing the organization in external events, profit sharing, among others.

From a social point of view, it is a fact that people take home their company problems and that they bring their personal problems to the workplace. To expect that a person can be physically in the office when having three personal issues to resolve and are mentally juggling to see how to get it done while being present to meet office corporate calendar entirely out of the question. If the personal and professional agendas are not balanced, that person will never be 100% focused on the company tasks, even being physically presents in the workplace.

Everything revolves around time management, the harmony of professional tasks and knowledgeable ability to delegate. There are companies that offer conciliation services from organizations so that they service to workers in personal aspects on request as part of a family support package. The organization hires a work-life services company to offer this support to employees who want to use them and consequently pay for the services. In this way, the person has full support from a single provider, at any time of the day, which makes it easier to run the home and family.

Irene Bustamante, president of Healthy Company and Search Inc., points out that "if the employee is feels cared for, not only the quality of their work will increase but also their quality care for the family private life will run smoothly." The America Best Employers guide publishes the ranking published by Glassdoor of companies in the United States that are excellent in offering support to their workforce as a strategic factor.

In the nineties, the European Institute of Social Capital (IECS) of the German government created the Work and Life Balance certification to establish the support standards of companies that offer conciliation services in Germany. This certification was considered compulsory for companies to have a basic element to ensure quality of life to the workforce.

In Spain, some of the thirty-two main organizations that provide conciliation services are: the International Court of Conciliation and Arbitration in Guipúzcoa, the Center for Conciliation, Mediation and Arbitration in Valencia and Nuria Chinchilla Consultores Asociados in Barcelona, among others. These institutions offer family support programs for childcare, for elderly and other dependents, concierge services (repairs, catering, shopping, laundry), mobility support (housing, cultural training, schools, language), legal and tax advice, early retirement programs, insurance, food vouchers, travel, and scholarships, among others to cover the family needs of any company employee.

One of the advantages of distance working is that it reduces the need for conciliation support services: both men and women are able to take over a large part of the activities that they are now forced to subcontract. It will also change the way of buying and consuming at home, which will force a total transformation of family service companies and force a radical change in the business globally, influencing in turn emerging opportunities such as employment, family business, and start-ups; the core of a new circular economy.

CHAPTER 23

Inclusion: The Cost of Discrimination

Its walls are not the limits of a company. A company begins with its suppliers of raw materials and services, and ends when its customers have destroyed its products or services. The most decisive factors that influence the success of the company generally come from beyond its limits, from local and global external environments. Thinking outside is a highly recommended practice for companies wanting to be present in future markets. Supplier partnership is the type of relationship to be developed. The Institute for Supply Management defines supplier partnership as: "a commitment over an extended time to work together to the mutual benefit of both parties, sharing relevant information and the risks and rewards of the relationship."

There are companies such as Procter and Gamble and Toyota, which often are cited as companies with a strong regard for partnering and collaboration. "We expect the best from our business partners, and we are focused on growing long-term relationships that are sustainable, innovative and create joint value," said Rick Hughes, P&G chief purchasing officer.

Therefore, it is equally critical to know how to integrate all external agents as part of the core business. Their developments influence the quality and of corporate products as well as its distinctive characteristics. As far as clients is concerned, the sense of belonging must be encouraged, as it will also determine the success and sustainability of the organization. Therefore, a macro-objective is to nurture the sense of belonging of clients, suppliers, administrations, social, and economic agents in general.

However, in Spain only fifteen percent of companies believe that considering suppliers and other external agents as partners of the organization is fundamental for the company. Ten percent consider it harmful to stimulate the interaction and collaboration between employees and external agents, considering that it does not have a positive benefit.

As to the inclusion of suppliers, Supplier Diversity was the pioneer organization in promoting the extension of the company inclusion policies to its suppliers, and thus ensuring the efficiency of the business process. This policy is a rich source of resources. Suppliers are pioneers in learning about new raw materials, technologies, colors, and design, which are the emerging trends and what can help the company to avoid discontinuity. Some important factors are:

- Information: it can contribute to the introduction of new materials, delivery and distribution systems that become key factors for innovation in the company and to keep its products and services young in changing environments.
- Competition: know the existence and strengths of emerging competitors which generally are also clients of the suppliers.
- Efficiency: create partnership with suppliers for both to benefit from costs reductions or process structuring.
- Logistics: rationalize systems related to stock availability.
- Financial conditions: build financial strategies based on trust and agreements that benefit both organizations.

Some companies that have joined Supplier Diversity project are Accenture, Corporate Express, Merrill Lynch, Adecco, Credit Lyonnaise, Pfizer, Hewlett-Packard, Williams Lea, Citigroup, IBM Cisco Systems, Deutsche Bank, Credit Suisse, Cristal Mayer, Goldman Sachs, and Squibb, among others.

Regarding the inclusion of clients, understanding their profiles represents the greatest challenge that companies face today and in the future. Thinking and acting glocal is an essential behavior to guarantee the future presence in the market, regardless the size of the organization.

A systematic monitoring of the increasingly diverse profile of its external agents and anticipating their new and changing needs constitutes a guideline for the sustainability of the organization. Even when the company is local, it will surely have the possibility of global clients and suppliers, either by physical presence or by virtual communication. The speed of change creates new clusters of consumers who previously had not required the company outputs. The ability to detect new target communities is essential for business sustainability. A systemic scenario is in constant and rapid evolution. Simultaneously, the transformational behavior of its agents does not leave room to wait for another to fill its place. Social, economic, technological, and political agents must anticipate and detect these needs to reinvent their business and thus meet emerging and diverse market needs.

It is therefore mandatory for the profile of the company workforce to match that of the clients and external agents, which does not mean that the company must have a statistical representation of employees of the different profiles of its consumer market; gender, nationalities, education levels and other relevant traits that are relevant to the overall target community. The workforce must have the capacity to interact with multiple cultures and profiles in order to effectively interact with the changing profiles of its external audiences. To this end, intercultural training becomes a key training activity of any institution wanting to succeed in the business world.

In Germany, Deutsche Bank carried out a demographic analysis of the age curve of its staff and compared it to the age of its clients. Then analyzed the investment portfolio of its clients according to their age. The result was that seventy percent of the bank liabilities came from clients over sixty-five years of age, in which age group there were no employees to accurately assess this very critical client base. A major and costly disconnection became very evident to the Diversity Council of the Bank, between the needs, priorities, and investment choice of customers due to their age, in relation to the attitude and advice of the employees who serviced their accounts. The bank agents were younger and with other priorities in the sale of financial services. Immediately, the bank created a program to attract retired employees with high quality skills and knowledge to advise senior clients who were invited to participate in investments planning meetings with senior clients. It is out of the question to propose long-term investment products, when the "long term" of a seventy-year-old client is probably tomorrow, five years away!

Although twenty percent of companies in Spain encourage their workers to seek and obtain information from the company related environment, there is still thirty-three percent who do not take advantage of the value of the inclusion of external agents to generate intelligent information that instruct corporate processes, systems, and overall decision making. The argument of the employers is that developing strategies is reserved for those responsible for the management of the company. Organizations need to assess the cost of not including their "partners" in their business process on their day-to-day operations and relationships, as cultural interaction can eliminate errors, improve deliveries, reduce stocks, develop innovation and increase benefits for both organizations.

Shareholders make possible the very existence of the company, as well as of its development and diversification projects. Shareholders not only finance the start-up of the company, but even more importantly, they finance its expansion, technology investment, contingencies and suitability by having financial resources available in the extremely aggressive present and future markets.

It is ethical to keep stakeholders informed of the diversity inclusion policies of all the publics of the organization. It is very convenient to established communication channels to inform relevant daily news, projects and activities launched by the company which gain public recognition. This strategy considerably increases the value of the organization.

It is vital to create partnership alliances with local administrations, not only regarding legislation and other economic issues, but also in the creation of jobs and contributions that the company can make that improves the quality of life of local municipality residents. Frequently, companies sponsor local day care centers, sports programs, technological support and social responsibility activities aimed at the most vulnerable sectors. It must be remembered that users buy the brand and the company, not just the product, and identify with those companies, no matter their size, that actively favor society. Administrations must support those business activities that not only create jobs, but also contribute to creating an inclusive social scenario.

A wine company in Catalonia made a commitment to ensure jobs for all persons with disabilities in the territory (a policy which the company has never announced publicly). This social policy has resulted in significant economic results. The company commits to create jobs for all disabled persons in the area. The population of immigrant workers at peak work seasons does not represent any problem for the local population. The entire permanent staff of the company, as well as the local population, has a high inclusive behavior, respect, and sense of belonging towards the company and its brand.

Two out of three companies in the United States offer childcare programs to their workers, because they experience that it is a great recruitment tool. Seven percent do it as corporate policy, according to the Society for Human Resource Management of National Studies of Employers in 2016. Companies such as Cisco and Patagonia lead this list. The Home Depot, based in Atlanta with 7,000 workers, even offers childcare services for children over six years old in partnership with local city councils for candidates who attend a recruiting interview.

Liverpool City Council operates six kindergartens and childcare centers in collaboration with local businesses to promote high-quality support for children and families. It is a policy that contributes to the employability of local talent. On the other hand, the Vancouver City Council announced on July 4, 2019, that it already had 2,300 places covered in childcare centers which it launched in partnership with public and private associations, as well as with city companies which financed the project. Thus, it contributes to the quality of life and raises the feeling of loyalty of residents, as well as of corporate agents.

CHAPTER 24

Measure and Evaluate:
What is not Measured is not Done

"What cannot be measured is not done." This is the wise corporate principle that governs diversity inclusion policy of SHELL. It is a wise statement that everyone in the company understands and shares. The application of this principle guarantees the financial and social efficiency with which projects are implemented in all areas of the company.

Establishing corporate policies instantly sets the indicators by which corporate results are to be measured and evaluated to propel the company towards leadership position today and in the future. Therefor it is mandatory, to measure the results of each diversity related program. Measuring and evaluating is a strategic practice. Identifies the actions that contribute the most to the bottom line. Decision-making then has valuable information that allows a wise allocation of the human and financial resources that will be assigned to those programs and projects that report higher profitability and greater impact for the organization.

Gender diversity is a business case for companies that know how to include and optimize this resource. In 2019, an extensive statistical analysis was carried out based on the historical movements of personnel (hire, promote, rotate) to assess how to achieve gender balance at senior management levels at medium term. The findings have focused on the recruitment and promotion of women. Progress has been made, globally, from eleven percent in 2004 to twenty-two percent in 2020. Gender diversity has always been a priority. Presently, fifty percent of PwC's global workforce is made up of women.

The Costs and Benefits of Diversity report, published by the CSES for the European Union, is a reference document that monitors the implementation of D&I policies as a business case, not only as a socially correct management strategy. These policies improve global management, because its people have the capacity to promote inter-culturality and to manage the changing needs of suppliers and customers. They also avoid the legal costs of the current legislation on anti-discrimination practices; fines that in many cases have a high cost. In addition, they guarantee leadership through early participation in new market segments for their products and services. These policies also contribute to reduce absenteeism and turnover while increasing the capacity for innovation and creativity of their people. Also helps to attract professionals with high skills and performance levels; as well as promoting the reputation of the organization, gain customer loyalty, while reinforcing its cultural values.

To establish strategies whose objective is to evaluate and measure the results of diversity inclusion programs, tangible and intangible indicators must be taken into consideration and used. Tangible indicators that can measure the results of each program are: employee surveys, cost and benefit indicators, historical reports, human resources database, market analysis, accounting results, balanced scorecards, among other. The intangible indicators measure the attitude of employees, customers and suppliers. They are generally carried out periodically to monitor behavioral and attitude changes of the overall target populations that makes up the company. The ultimate goal of any business strategy is to master the parameters that lead to achieving high returns on investment, whether large or SMEs companies.

While eighty-three percent of international companies measure the staff satisfaction index, only fifty percent of Spanish companies do so. Spanish companies measure more customer turnover and satisfaction. ROI is monitored constantly in international companies. However, there is a wide range of measurement systems available to organizations that want to measure the impact of their D&I actions, such as:

- Employee surveys: to know the level of satisfaction of the persons that make up the workforce, which determines their contribution to the effectiveness of the organization.
- Cost benefit indicators: they respond to corporate objectives and assess the level of compliance that the strategy helps to achieve.
- Status reports that facilitates periodical evaluation of the degree of compliance of each program in order to introduce timely modifications.
- Databases of Human Resources profiles that indicate the level of compliance in promoting a diverse and inclusive workforce.
- Forecast and trend analysis that anticipate the changes that may arise and can affect the organizational management strategy.
- Market analysis and research, which detects the new cultural and demographic profiles of new consumers, which will determine the needs for

innovative characteristics of products and services that the organization must develop.

- Certification that proves respect for the equal rights of its people regarding their compensation.

"No matter where your company is located or what industry it works in, it has the power to make a real difference." The Equal Salary Foundation, founded in 2010, is an organization that certifies equal pay between men and women. The certification was developed by Véronique Goy Veenhuys in collaboration with the University of Geneva and PwC. To obtain this certification, companies have to justify and meet a four stages process: analysis of salaries which gap cannot be higher than five percent audit the equal rights and treatment policy related to all persons of the organization; a certification issued stating that the company operates with equal rights and pay; and live up to this certification valid for three years. Esther Mut, partner of PwC, explains how the company has contributed to the global implementation of the certification, which currently has eighty-four accredited organizations such as: Cartier, UBS, Gruppo Credito Emiliano, Ferrari, Philip Morris International, Lyreco Switzerland, Romande Energie, and Banque Cantonale du Valais.

The use of the balanced scorecard as a management tool already provides the company with information on the economic performance of each project. The impact of each program is measured independently, in order first to identify which actions make a higher contribution and then identify the global contribution of the corporate inclusion policy. The use of indicators is always a very efficient way to measure and evaluate the actions designed and implemented by everyone in the organization.

It is about clearly establishing the corporate objective for which the program is designed, which then allows to identify the indicators that will measure the results of the project and its economic contribution to the company. If a corporate objective were, for example, the rationalization of distribution costs, any distribution-related inclusion program that is implemented will measure its results based on the reduction achieved in those costs. The same principle would be applied in the case of designing inclusion projects to retain customers or if the aim is to maintain technological leadership; or if the intention is to increase the capacity for innovation or the early identification of new customer profiles. In this last case the statistical research will focus on the distribution of the different demographic and cultural profiles of the consumer population. The results then are measured and compared with the statistics of previous years in order to identify whether the marketing policy is attracting new clients for the given diverse profiles the organization is aiming to service.

Thus, it is very effective to measure and evaluate comparing with previous programs to know exactly what has been the contribution of that specific action or project. The tangible values for example would be the number of hours reduced in the distribution process, the number of new customers attracted, and new technologies developed. And the intangible values would be the level of satisfaction of new customers or of employee´s contentment regarding the corporate training methodologies, or the level to which the workforce use new ones, and the number of incorporated technologies, among others.

Some examples of costs and benefits from the cases already mentioned show their contribution to corporate objectives and the organizational results.

Wine Company

- Corporate objective. A wine company in Spain set itself the objective of eliminating the costs of conflicts created by strikes of workers in protest for the temporary hiring of immigrants at specific harvest times.
- Strategy. The designed strategy was to develop an essential social action for the quality of life of the of the region population. Support and work were organized for all people with disabilities in the region. In fact, taking into account that much of the work in the region is created by this company, most of the employees are relatives or acquaintances of people with disabilities in the area.
- Social result. Elimination of labor conflicts, reduced absenteeism and low turnover of the workforce. Massive respect and recognition from all the local population.
- Cost of the program. The cost of the project design and the cost of the infrastructure for the care and employment creation of the community of people with disabilities of the region.
- Profit result. The project has eliminated strikes caused by the discrimination of immigrant workers and, therefore this corporate commitment has eliminated this historical economic and social costs. It has also won the appreciation and recognition of the population of the area as well as of the local administrations.

Xerox Corporation

- Corporate objective. In 2000, Richard Thoman, the then CEO of the company, presented the project goal to increase the effectiveness of customer service.
- Strategy. Establish a network of 3,000 volunteer workers in distance work groups. A workstation was established in the home of each employee and one coordinator is assigned per group. Training was given the group leaders and project members in inclusion and communication.
- Social results. Ninety-seven percent employee satisfaction was achieved, attracting best talent. The environmental impact was reduced given the reduces mobility of 3,000 persons.
- Economic results. Customer service volume tripled. Absenteeism and turnover were eliminated.

Deutsche Bank

Corporate objective. Increase the number of clients.

- Strategy. It was published in the press that bank employees of the LGTBI group service personally clients who requested any type of service form the bank.
- Social results. Clear message of inclusion of diversity. Large number of new clients were attracted. Internal respect for the LGTBI collective if the workforce increased.
- Economic results. Spectacular increase in new accounts and business volume.

The labor force is not measured by its number and even less by its presence in the offices of companies or institutions. It is measured by the value of their contribution to the results of the organization, on the one hand, and by the employee cost each person has for the organization on the other hand.

It is essential for the organization to identify the right indicators to measure both factors that respond to its accounting and financial system, as well as the information it keeps regarding the behavior of each member of the workforce. This very valuable information portraits the value of the workforce profile, regarding their behavior in the different inclusive programs of the company. The cost and value of workers is a determining factor to take into account when calculating the amount and type of remuneration, promotion, rotation and turnover of members of the workforce.

The employee cost must include not only salary, as well as incentives, training and taxes, but also the cost of infrastructure. The value of the workforce is also determined by their ability to generate business opportunities, due to their inclusive behavior of diversity towards the rest of the company population. It is essential to assess their behavior to reduce internal and external conflicts, as well as their ability to generate innovation in the entity.

Creating a model that reflects the employee value of the members of the workforce is a very powerful tool particularly in moments of promotion and of assigning responsibilities at corporate decision-making levels.

CHAPTER 25

Cost of No Inclusion:
Cost of Not Managing Diversity

The diversity inclusion policies generate a transformation of the cultural behavior of all the members of the organization. This inclusive culture not only benefits the taskforce of the company, but expands its action to all the external agents that interact with the institution. The respect for diverse profiles in the work environment and in the general environment influences the sustainable creation of a socio-economic scenario. Inclusion also increases the ability to hold responsibility for the results of the organization and to develop a genuine sense of belonging of its peoples to the organization.

The benefits that the diversity inclusion policies and programs generate for the corporation world are multiple:

- Empowers the entire workforce of the organization to stimulate creativity, innovation and efficiency.
- Guarantees the creation of an inclusive work environment that encourages belonging to the company and reducing costs of absenteeism, turnover, lost and wasted time.
- Eliminates or reduces conflicts.
- Promotes time management that allows harmonizing professional and personal life of all members of the organization.
- Eliminates legal costs of discrimination.
- Sustains the development of the organization towards the future by building a workforce that reflects the profile of its local and global external publics.
- Fosters constant innovation in order achieve sustainability in fast and changing scenarios.
- Redesigns corporate objectives and policies in constantly changing and vulnerable markets.

The costs of not managing the inclusion of diversities are not affordable for any type of institution that wants to maintain a sustainable and leadership position in this century turbulent and changing scenarios. Some of the costs a company has to confront as a result of not being able to manage the inclusion of diverse profiles of its peoples:

- **Loss of talent recruitment**: talented professionals only choose environments in which they can contribute with their ideas and initiatives to build a dynamic and sustainable company.
- **Productivity and effectiveness**: The cases and good practices illustrated in the book strongly prove that an inclusive diverse workforce makes specific contributions to the productivity and effectiveness of organizations. An integrated workforce that embraces and respects the differences of other stakeholders empowers the capacity to increase the value chain, in order to operate with maximum efficiency. Win the loyalty of external customers: losing this value is equivalent to losing the value of the entire business. Only when the workforce reflects the diversity profile of its external agents, can the organization respond and anticipate the changing needs of its audiences; whether that of clients, suppliers, or institutions of the administrations. The external audience of any organization today and in the future is made up of people from all over the world, who condition bring in new parameters that influence all types of business activities.
- **Access to financing**: organizations have a constant need to access to financial resources, to finance cutting-edge technology, research that can make the difference in their sector, expansion or restructuring projects that guarantee the sustainability of the institution, alliances, or takeovers which complementarity can multiply corporate benefits. It is compulsory for companies to have constant and reliable access to financial resources as their survival depends of constantly reinventing its business objectives and innovation schemes in order to hold leadership positions in uncertain and changing environments. These sources should be integrated as core assets to the company structure.
- **Legal costs**: litigations always have a double cost for the organization; the financial cost and the intangible cost due to loss of image. In the case of legal procedures for discrimination issues, the fines can be multimillionaire besides the costly loss of credibility in the market. Since

2011, as mentioned earlier DG Justice established strict antidiscrimination legislation to be complied by the twenty-seven member states of the European Union.

In 2011, the National Competition Commission (CNC) fined for more than 51 million euros seven companies that manufactures of professional hairdressing products as well as the National Association of Perfumes and Cosmetics (Stanpa) for implementing and maintaining discriminatory measures against community of the black community in the European Union. The sanctioned companies were L'Oréal Spain (23.2 million euros), Productos Cosméticos Wella (12 million euros), The Colomer Group Spain (8.7 million euros), Eugene Perma Spain (2.88 million euros), Cosmética Cosbar-Montibello (2.55 million euros), Lendan Cosmetics (1 million euros) and DSP Haircare Products (299,000 euros). Company executives were also fined for a total of 900,000 euros). L´Oréal launched a campaign to its entire workforce in Europe of training seminars, "La Beauté de la Différence," to create awareness and corporate commitment towards diversity management policy under the direct leadership of the CEO and the board of directors. This campaign also reached the external public of clients, suppliers and administrations of the different countries of the European Union.

The U.S. Equal Employment Opportunity Commission (EEOC) enforces antidiscrimination laws. A company accused of discrimination or harassment, can potentially face a long and costly legal.

Amazon was fined (877 million dollars) and WhatsApp (255 million dollars for data processing practices. Google was fined cookies consent procedures. H&M was fined (41 million dollars for illegal monitoring of several hundred employees. TIM Italian Telecom was fined (35 million dollars) for over aggressive marketing strategies. British Airways was fined (26 million dollars) for breaching 400,000 customers' payment card information. Marriott Hotels was fined (23.8 million dollars) for compromise personal date of 484 million guests. Wal-Mart was fined for over 1.000 million dollars for discriminating practices of gender, age, ethnicity, salary gap, and other to its 1.3 million workers; settlement was reached with the mediation of the US government to avoid bankruptcy.

- **Loss of corporate image**: any error in dealing with the demographic and intercultural differences of the company stands for a loss of business volume, customers, and purchasing power.

The same occurs with suppliers, shareholders, and administrations. The capacity of innovation and repositioning in the markets, is crucial for the company to survive in vulnerable and changing scenarios. Winning over and retaining the loyalty of its external agents is very costly; but can be easily lost if the organization and all its people do not truly commitment to operate with an inclusive behavior of respect towards the differences of all its community of workers as well as of external agents.

On November 16, 2000, Coca-Cola chose to pay $192.5 million to 2,000 Black employees who sued the corporation for discriminatory practices and reached settlement before going to trial. Since then, Coca-Cola has projected in all its advertising campaigns clear inclusive messages: spots and photographs of people of all ages, ethnicities, and cultures sharing the pleasure of drinking Coca-Cola. But it does not always succeed. In 2019, the Pest County Consumer Protection Department in Hungary fined the company for 500,000 forints (just over 1,500 euros) for the "Love is Love" campaign, which although it aimed at being pro-LGTBI featuring two young women holding hands, aroused the anger of the entire homosexual community in the country.

Diversity management, as has been proven throughout this book, is a corporate policy and strategy that requires:

- Mechanisms that must be used by all the managers of the organization responsible for corporate results.
- An effective measurement and evolution system that allows resources to be allocated to those actions that can contribute more effectively to the tangible and intangible results of the company.

Forecasting tools and trend analysis of future scenarios constitutes a key exercise for the company to structure the profile of its workforce in order to position itself with a competitive edge in VUCA scenarios. The future started yesterday. The talent profile the company needs tomorrow needs to be attracted and retained today.

The social inclusion of diversity is managed not because it is a responsibility that the company has towards society; but it is the responsibility of the company to create, direct, and sustain a profitable economic organization that provides products or services to an increasingly globalized and diverse population and then the organization has the financial resources that allows it to remunerate the talented diverse workforce necessary to ensure its sustainability. The company mission is not creating jobs. A company is set up to carry out the vision and mission of those entrepreneurs who take the risk of investing in a specific business project. The corporate aim is to operate with a healthy bottom line in order to comply with all the costs related to the business activity: reward shareholders, pay employees, production, logistics, technology, infrastructure, overheads, taxes, and of course, profits,

The organization should create alliances with its external publics, which includes suppliers and public administrations. Leveraging job creation of local residents, for example is a very powerful argument to establish projects co-financed by the local administration, such as childcare centers, or training programs.

On the other hand, financing projects of a social nature aimed at less favored segments of the population is not the responsibility of the company; it is the responsibility of public administrations, to whom residents pays through taxes the funds governments need to fight against these discriminatory behaviors, improve education and health services, and build a better quality of life for all residents. Companies undertake social oriented projects to satisfy and win over their audiences, to make a contribution to an increasingly unequal population. Mixed races is the prevalent ethnic profile of the world population today and towards the future. The winner of the 2021 US Women Open was Gemma Raducano, British citizen of Roumanian father and Chinese mother, over Leylah Fernandez, Canadian citizen of Ecuadorian father and Filipino mother.

Companies that perform with inclusive policies and which sponsor social interest projects should be given recognition and be awarded. Rewarding rather than penalizing is a culture which should be exercised by all types of organizations, which will have higher rates of success when it comes to developing social and economic projects with the business world.

The inclusion of the diversity of people is managed because it is a business case, and it is vital for the sustainability of the companies that are part of the circular economy that identifies the current socio-economic system and the Fourth Industrial Revolution of the coming years. It is managed to adapt its strategies to the realities of the highly diverse and global markets. It is managed to guarantee sustainable development to organization as they advance towards future scenarios, in constant change, vulnerable, uncertain, convulsive, ambiguous, and diverse.

Unesco Universal Declaration on Cultural Diversity

"The cultural wealth of the world is its diversity in dialogue." The UNESCO Universal Declaration on Cultural Diversity was adopted unanimously in a most unusual context. It came in the wake of the events of 11 September 2001, and the UNESCO General Conference, which was meeting for its 31st session, was the first ministerial-level meeting to be held after those terrible events. It was an opportunity for States to reaffirm their conviction that intercultural dialogue is the best guarantee of peace and to reject outright the theory of the inevitable clash of cultures and civilizations. Such a wide-ranging instrument is a first for the international community. It raises cultural diversity to the level of "the common heritage of humanity," "as necessary for humankind as biodiversity is for nature" and makes its defense an ethical imperative in dissociable from respect for the dignity of the individual.

The Declaration aims both to preserve cultural diversity as a living, and thus renewable treasure that must not be perceived as being unchanging heritage but as a process guaranteeing the survival of humanity; and to prevent segregation and fundamentalism which, in the name of cultural differences, would sanctify those differences and so counter the message of the Universal Declaration of Human Rights. The Universal Declaration makes it clear that each individual must acknowledge not only otherness in all its forms but also the plurality of his or her own identity, within societies that are themselves plural. Only in this way can cultural diversity be preserved as an adaptive process and as a capacity for expression, creation and innovation. The debate between those countries which would like to defend cultural goods and services "which, as vectors of identity, values and meaning, must not be treated as mere commodities or consumer goods", and those which would hope to promote cultural rights has thus been surpassed, with the two approaches brought together by the Declaration, which has highlighted the causal link uniting two complementary attitudes. One cannot exist without the other.

The Declaration, accompanied by the main lines of an action plan, can be an outstanding tool for development, capable of humanizing globalization. Of course, it lays down not instructions but general guidelines to be turned into ground-breaking policies by Member States in their specific contexts, in partnership with the private sector and civil society. This Declaration, which

sets against inward-looking fundamentalism the prospect of a more open, creative and democratic world, is now one of the founding texts of the new ethics promoted by UNESCO in the early twenty-first century.
My hope is that one day it may acquire the same force as the Universal Declaration of Human Rights.

Koïchiro Matsuura Director-General

2 November 2001

THE GENERAL CONFERENCE, Committed to the full implementation of the human rights and fundamental freedoms proclaimed in the Universal Declaration of Human Rights and other universally recognized legal instruments, such as the two International Covenants of 1966 relating respectively to civil and political rights and to economic, social and cultural rights, Recalling that the Preamble to the Constitution of UNESCO affirms "that the wide diffusion of culture, and the education of humanity for justice and liberty and peace are indispensable to the dignity of man and constitute a sacred duty which all the nations must fulfil in a spirit of mutual assistance and concern," Further recalling Article I of the Constitution, which assigns to UNESCO among other purposes that of recommending "such international agreements as may be necessary to promote the free flow of ideas by word and image,"

Referring to the provisions relating to cultural diversity and the exercise of cultural rights in the international instruments enacted by UNESCO,

1. Reaffirming that culture should be regarded as the set of distinctive spiritual, material, intellectual and emotional features of society or a social group, and that it encompasses, in addition to art and literature, lifestyles, ways of living together, value systems, traditions and beliefs,

2. Noting that culture is at the heart of contemporary debates about identity, social cohesion, and the development of a knowledge-based economy, Affirming that respect for the diversity of cultures, tolerance, dialogue and cooperation, in a climate of mutual trust and understanding are among the best guarantees of international peace and security, Aspiring to greater solidarity on the basis of recognition of cultural diversity, of awareness of the unity of humankind, and of the development of intercultural exchanges, Considering that the process of globalization, facilitated by the rapid development of new information and communication tech-

nologies, though representing a challenge for cultural diversity, creates the conditions for renewed dialogue among cultures and civilizations,

Aware of the specific mandate which has been entrusted to UNESCO, within the United Nations system, to ensure the preservation and promotion of the fruitful diversity of cultures, Proclaims the following principles and adopts the present Declaration:

1. Among which, in particular, the Florence Agreement of 1950 and its Nairobi Protocol of 1976, the Universal Copyright Convention of 1952, the Declaration of the Principles of International Cultural Cooperation of 1966, the Convention on the Means of Prohibiting and Preventing the Illicit Import, Export and Transfer of Ownership of Cultural Property of 1970, the Convention for the Protection of the World Cultural and Natural Heritage of 1972, the Declaration on Race and Racial Prejudice of 1978, the Recommendation concerning the Status of the Artist of 1980, and the Recommendation on Safeguarding Traditional Culture and Folklore of 1989.

2. This definition is in line with the conclusions of the World Conference on Cultural Policies (MONDIACULT, Mexico City, 1982), of the World Commission on Culture and Development (Our Creative Diversity, 1995), and of the Intergovernmental Conference on Cultural Policies for Development (Stockholm, 1998).

UNESCO Universal Declaration on Cultural Diversity Identity, Diversity, and Pluralism

ARTICLE 1. Cultural diversity: the common heritage of humanity. Culture takes diverse forms across time and space. This diversity is embodied in the uniqueness and plurality of the identities of the groups and societies making up humankind. As a source of exchange, innovation and creativity, cultural diversity is as necessary for humankind as biodiversity is for nature. In this sense, it is the common heritage of humanity and should be recognized and affirmed for the benefit of present and future generations.

ARTICLE 2. From cultural diversity to cultural pluralism. In our increasingly diverse societies, it is essential to ensure harmonious interaction among people and groups with plural, varied and dynamic cultural identities as well as their willingness to live together. Policies for the inclusion and participation of all citizens are guarantees of social cohesion, the vitality of civil society and peace. Thus defined, cultural pluralism gives policy expression to the reality of cultural diversity. Indi sociable from a democratic framework, cultural pluralism is conducive to cultural exchange and to the flourishing of creative capacities that sustain public life.

ARTICLE 3. Cultural diversity as a factor in development. Cultural diversity widens the range of options open to everyone; it is one of the roots of development, understood not simply in terms of economic growth, but also as a means to achieve a more satisfactory intellectual, emotional, moral and spiritual existence.

Cultural Diversity and Human Rights

ARTICLE 4. Human rights as guarantees of cultural diversity. The defense human dignity. It implies a commitment to human rights and fundamental freedoms, in particular the rights of persons belonging to minorities and those of indigenous peoples. No one may invoke cultural diversity to infringe upon human rights guaranteed by international law, nor to limit their scope.

ARTICLE 5. Cultural rights as an enabling environment for cultural diversity. Cultural rights are an integral part of human rights, which are universal, indivisible and interdependent. The flourishing of creative diversity requires the full implementation of cultural rights as defined in Article 27 of the Universal Declaration of Human Rights and in Articles 13 and 15 of the International Covenant on Economic, Social and Cultural Rights. All persons have therefore the right to express themselves and to create and disseminate their work in the language of their choice, and particularly in their mother tongue; all persons are entitled to quality education and training that fully respect their cultural identity; and all persons have the right to participate in the cultural life of their choice and conduct their own cultural practices, subject to respect for human rights and fundamental freedoms.

ARTICLE 6. Towards access for all to cultural diversity. While ensuring the free flow of ideas by word and image care should be exercised that all cultures can express themselves and make themselves known. Freedom of expression, media pluralism, multilingualism, equal access to art and to scientific and technological knowledge, including in digital form, and the possibility for all cultures to have access to the means of expression and dissemination are the guarantees of cultural diversity.

Cultural Diversity and Creativity

ARTICLE 7. Cultural heritage as the wellspring of creativity. Creation draws on the roots of cultural tradition, but flourishes in contact with other cultures. For this reason, heritage in all its forms must be preserved, enhanced and handed on to future generations as a record of human experience and aspirations, so as to foster creativity in all its diversity and to inspire genuine dialogue among cultures.

ARTICLE 8. Cultural goods and services: commodities of a unique kind. In the face of present-day economic and technological change, opening up vast prospects for creation and innovation, particular attention must be paid to the diversity of the supply of creative work, to due recognition of the rights of authors and artists and to the specificity of cultural goods and services which, as vectors of identity, values and meaning, must not be treated as mere commodities or consumer goods.

ARTICLE 9. Cultural policies as catalysts of creativity. While ensuring the free circulation of ideas and works, cultural policies must create conditions conducive to the production and dissemination of diversified cultural goods and services through cultural industries that have the means to assert themselves at the local and global level. It is for each State, with due regard to its international obligations, to define its cultural policy and to implement it through the means it considers fit, whether by operational support or appropriate regulations.

Cultural Diversity and International Solidarity

ARTICLE 10. Strengthening capacities for creation and dissemination worldwide. In the face of current imbalances in flows and exchanges of cultural goods and services at the global level, it is necessary to reinforce international cooperation and solidarity aimed at enabling all countries, especially developing countries and countries in transition, to establish cultural industries that are viable and competitive at national and international level.

ARTICLE 11. Building partnerships between the public sector, the private sector and civil society. Market forces alone cannot guarantee the preservation and promotion of cultural diversity, which is the key to sustainable human development. From this perspective, the pre-eminence of public policy, in partnership with the private sector and civil society, must be reaffirmed.

ARTICLE 12. The role of UNESCO, by virtue of its mandate and functions, has the responsibility to:

a- Promote the incorporation of the principles set out in the present Declaration into the development strategies drawn up within the various intergovernmental bodies;

b- Serve as a reference point and a forum where States, international governmental and non-governmental organizations, civil society and the private sector may join together in elaborating concepts, objectives and policies in favor of cultural diversity;

c- Pursue its activities in standard-setting, awareness raising and capacity-building in the areas related to the present Declaration within its fields of competence; d- Facilitate the implementation of the Action Plan, the main lines of which are appended to the present Declaration.

UNESCO Universal Declaration on Cultural Diversity

1. Deepening the international debate on questions relating to cultural diversity, particularly in respect of its links with development and its impact on policy-making, at both national and international level; taking forward notably consideration of the advisability of an international legal instrument on cultural diversity.

2. Advancing in the definition of principles, standards and practices, on both the national and the international levels, as well as of awareness-raising modalities and patterns of cooperation, that are most conducive to the safeguarding and promotion of cultural diversity.

3. Fostering the exchange of knowledge and best practices in regard to cultural pluralism with a view to facilitating, in diversified societies, the inclusion and participation of persons and groups from varied cultural backgrounds.

4. Making further headway in understanding and clarifying the content of cultural rights as an integral part of human rights.

5. Safe guarding the linguistic heritage of humanity and giving support to expression, creation and dissemination in the greatest possible number of languages.

6. Encouraging linguistic diversity – while respecting the mother tongue – at all levels of education, MAIN LINES OF AN ACTION PLAN FOR THE IMPLEMENTATION OF THE UNESCO UNIVERSAL DECLARATION ON CULTURAL DIVERSITY wherever possible, and fostering the learning of several languages from the earliest age.

7. Promoting through education an awareness of the positive value of cultural diversity and improving to this end both curriculum design and teacher education.

8. Incorporating where appropriate, traditional pedagogies into the education process with a view to preserving and making full use of culturally appropriate methods of communication and transmission of knowledge.

9. Encouraging "digital literacy" and ensuring greater mastery of the new information and communication technologies, which should be seen both as educational discipline and as pedagogical tools capable of enhancing the effectiveness of educational services.

10. Promoting linguistic diversity in cyberspace and encouraging universal access through the global network to all information in the public domain.

11. Countering the digital divide, in close cooperation in relevant United Nations system organizations, by fostering access by the developing countries to the new technologies, by helping them to master information technologies and by facilitating the digital dissemination of endogenous cultural products and access by those countries to the educational, cultural and scientific digital resources available worldwide.

The Member States commit themselves to taking appropriate steps to disseminate widely the "UNESCO Universal Declaration on Cultural Diversity" and to encourage its effective application, in particular by cooperating with a view to achieving the following objectives:

12. Encouraging the production, safeguarding and dissemination of diversified contents in the media and global information networks and, to that end, promoting the role of public radio and television services in the development of audiovisual productions of good quality, in particular by fostering the establishment of cooperative mechanisms to facilitate their distribution.

13. Formulating policies and strategies for the preservation and enhancement of the cultural and natural heritage, notably the oral and intangible cultural heritage, and combating illicit traffic in cultural goods and services.

14. Respecting and protecting traditional knowledge, in particular that of indigenous peoples; recognizing the contribution of traditional knowledge, particularly with regard to environmental protection and the management of natural resources and fostering synergies between modern science and local knowledge.

15. Fostering the mobility of creators, artists, researchers, scientists and intellectuals and the development of international research programmers and partnerships, while striving to preserve and enhance the creative capacity of developing countries and countries in transition.

16. Ensuring protection of copyright and related rights in the interest of the development of contemporary creativity and fair remuneration for creative work, while at the same time upholding a public right of access to culture, in accordance with Article 27 of the Universal Declaration of Human Rights.

17. Assisting in the emergence or consolidation of cultural industries in the developing countries and countries in transition and, to this end, cooperating in the development of the necessary infrastructures and skills, fostering the emergence of viable local markets, and facilitating access for the cultural products of those countries to the global market and international distribution networks.

18. Developing cultural policies, including operational support arrangements and/or appropriate regulatory frameworks, designed to promote the principles

enshrined in this Declaration, in accordance with the international obligations incumbent upon each State.

19. Involving all sectors of civil society closely in framing of public policies aimed at safeguarding and promoting cultural diversity.

20. Recognizing and encouraging the contribution that the private sector can make to enhancing cultural diversity and facilitating, to that end, the establishment of forums for dialogue between the public sector and the private sector. The Member States recommend that the Director-General take the objectives set forth in this Action Plan into account in the implementation of UNESCO's programmers and communicate it to institutions of the United Nations system and to other intergovernmental and non-governmental organizations concerned with a view to enhancing the synergy of actions in favor of cultural diversity.